BASS RECORDED VERSIONS

BEST OF MARCUS MILLER

Music transcriptions by Chris Kringel, Andy Schanz and David Stocker
Editorial assistance provided by Nick DePinna
Cover photo by Joke Schot

ISBN 978-1-4234-0433-0

HAL•LEONARD®
CORPORATION
7777 W. Bluemound Rd. P.O. Box 13819 Milwaukee, WI 53213

Visit Hal Leonard Online at
www.halleonard.com

CONTENTS

from Miles Davis - *Amandla*

Big Time

By Marcus Miller

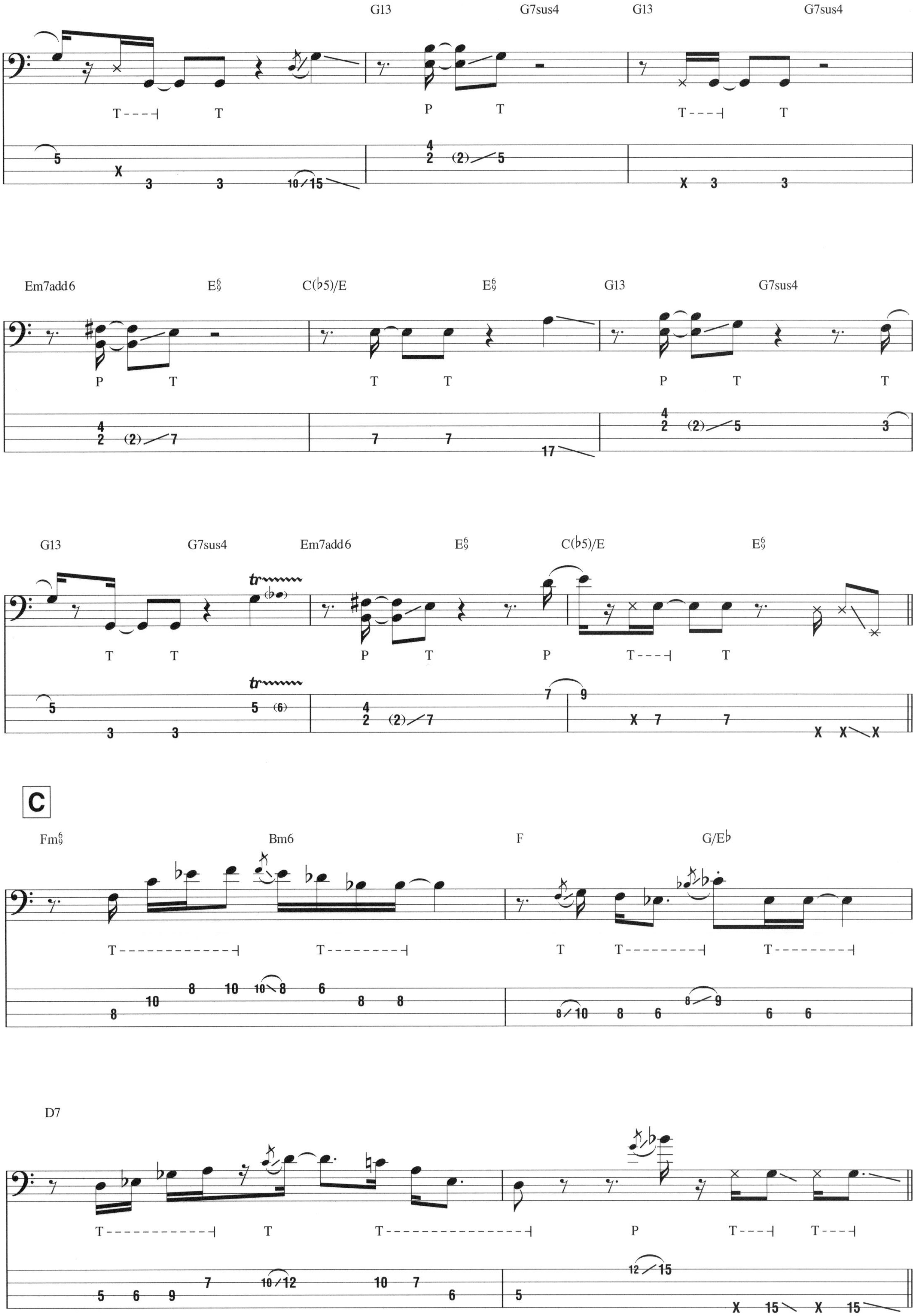
G13 G7sus4 G13 G7sus4
Em7add6 E6/9 C(♭5)/E E6/9 G13 G7sus4
G13 G7sus4 Em7add6 E6/9 C(♭5)/E E6/9
C
Fm6/9 Bm6 F G/E♭
D7

D
G13 G7sus4 G13 G7sus4
T T P T T P T P T
Em7add6 E6/9 C(♭5)/E E6/9 E5 G5
P T P T T T P T P
E5 G5
T T P T T T T
E
E5 G5 E5 G5
P T T P T T P T P
G7sus4
T T T T T P T T P T T P

G13
G7sus4
G13
G7sus4
Em7add6
E6/9
C(♭5)/E
E6/9
G13
G7sus4
G13
G7sus4
8va
loco
Em7add6
E6/9
C(♭5)/E
E6/9

F
Fm6/9
Bm6
F
G/E♭
D7
G13
G7sus4
G13
G7sus4
Em7add6
E6/9
C(♭5)/E
E6/9
G
Em

H
8va

8va
loco
I
E5 G5
E5 G5
J
G13 G7sus4 G13 G7sus4
Em7add6 E6/9 C(♭5)/E E6/9
G13 G7sus4 G13 G7sus4

Em7add6
E6/9
C(♭5)/E
E6/9
K
E5
G5
E5
G5
E5
G5
E5
G5
E5
G5
E5
G5
E5
G5

E5 G5
E5 G5 E5 G5
E5 G5
Begin fade
E5 G5 E5 G5
Fade out
E5 G5

from *Free*

Blast

By Marcus Miller

Basses 1 - 4: Drop D tuning:
(low to high) D-A-D-G

Bass 5: Drop D tuning:
(low to high) D-A-D-G-C

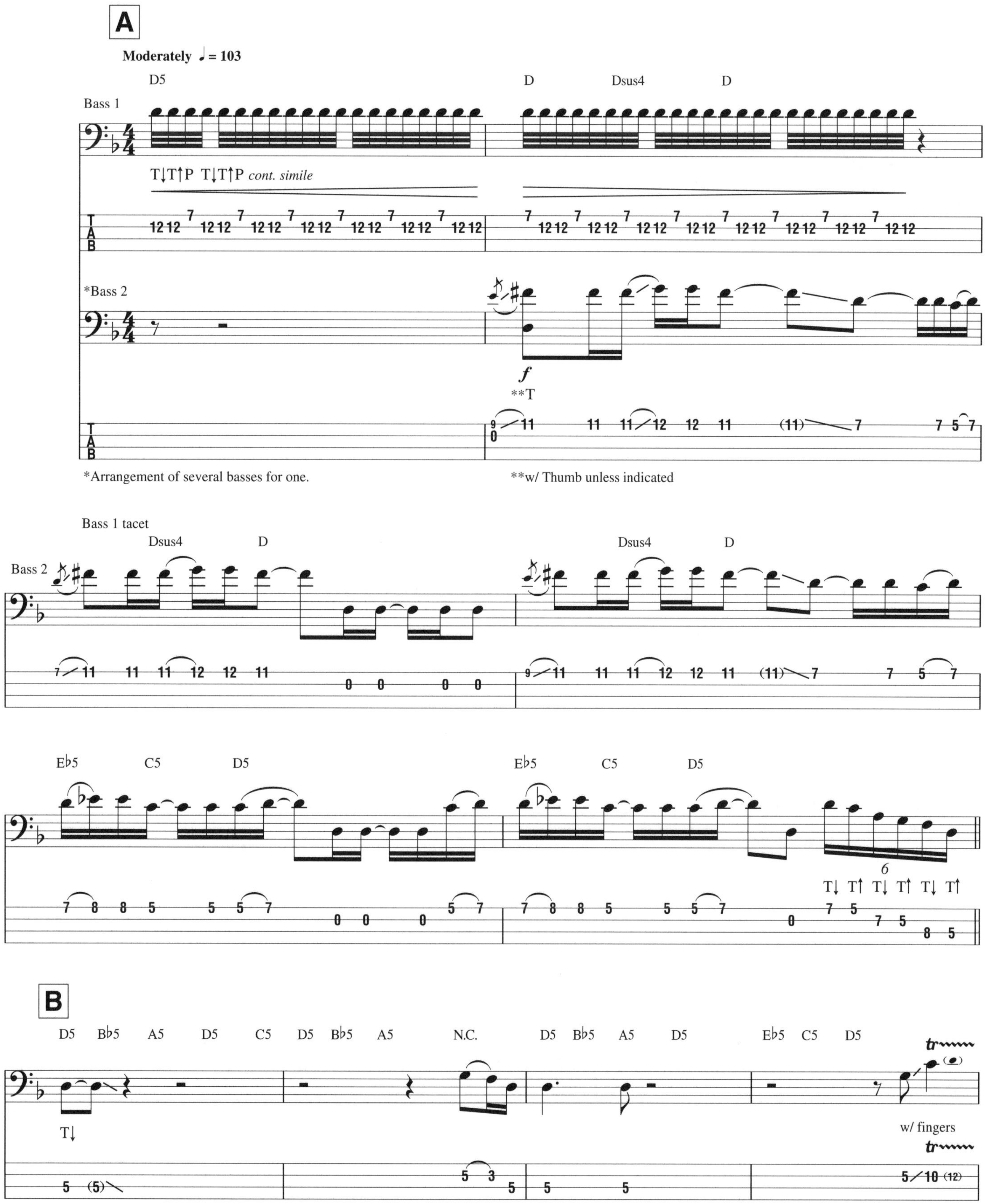

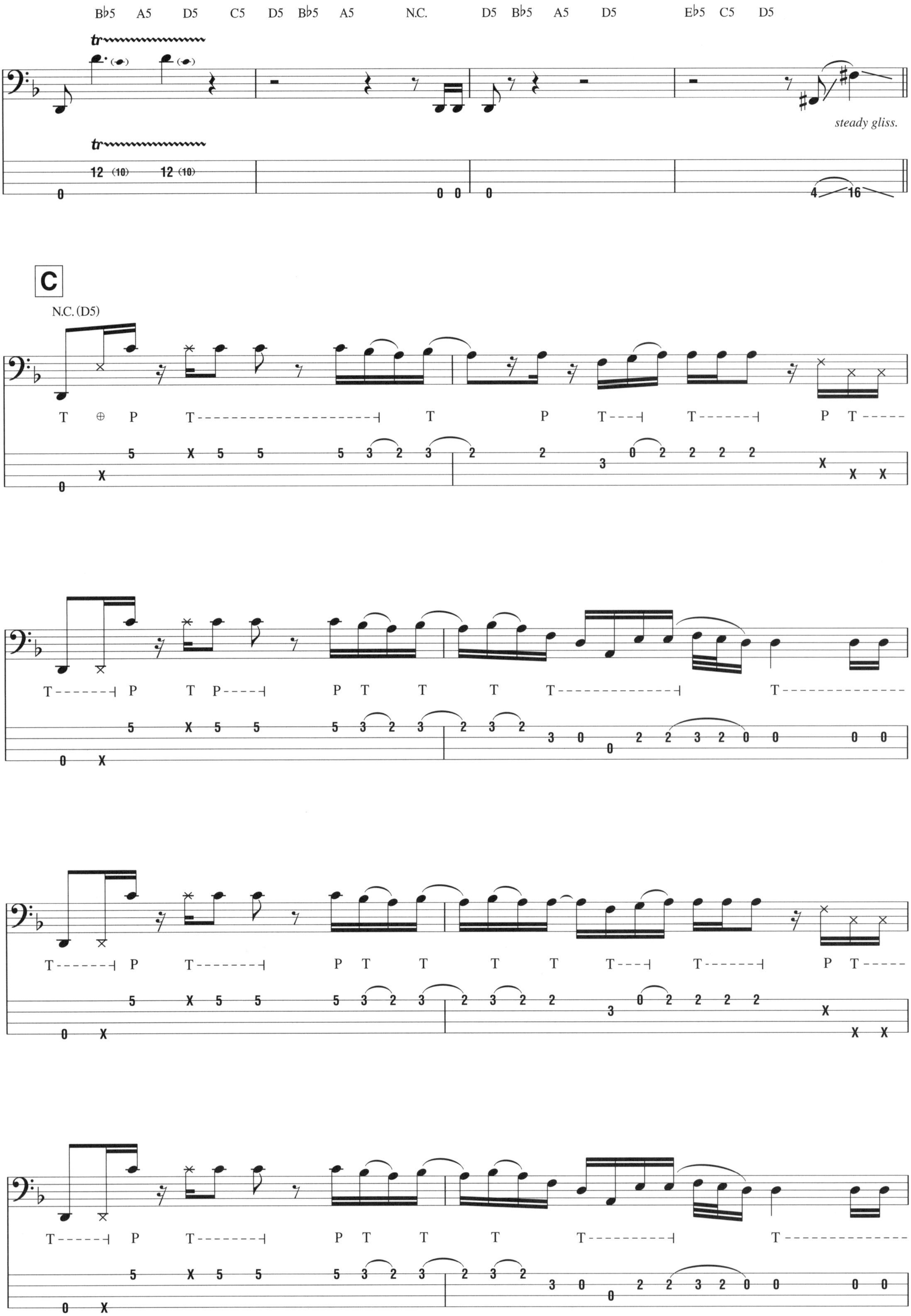
B♭5 A5 D5 C5 D5 B♭5 A5 N.C. D5 B♭5 A5 D5 E♭5 C5 D5
tr
steady gliss.
C
N.C. (D5)

D
D5 B♭5 A5 D5 C5 D5 B♭5 A5 N.C. D5 B♭5 A5 D5

Eb5 C5 D5 Bb5 A5 D5 C5 D5 Bb5 A5 N.C.
D5 Bb5 A5 D5 Eb5 C5 D5
E
N.C. (D5)

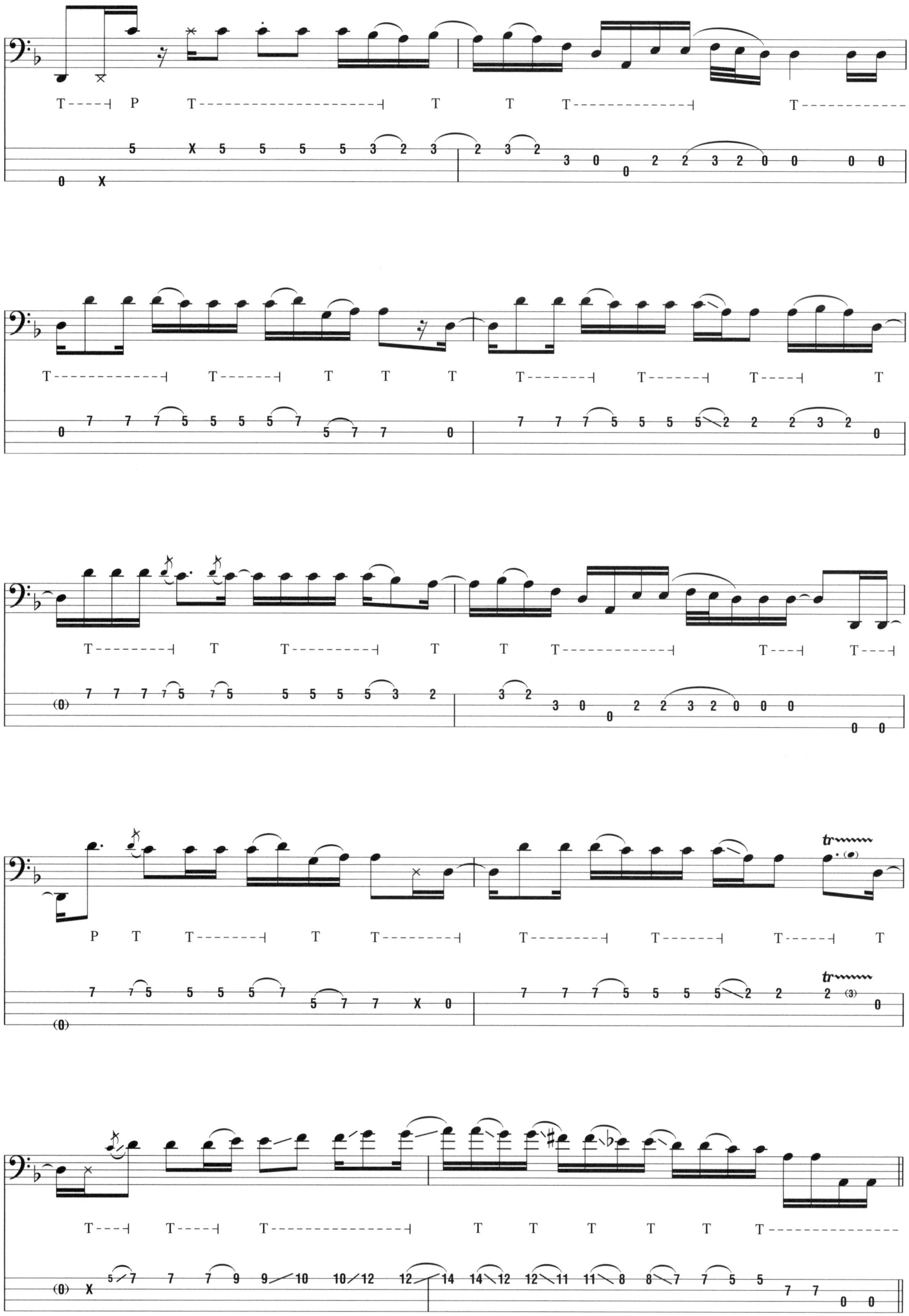

F
D5 B♭5 A5 D5 C5 D5 B♭5 A5 N.C. D5 B♭5 A5 D5
E♭5 C5 D5 D5 B♭5 A5 D5 C5 D5 B♭5 A5 N.C.
D5 B♭5 A5 D5 E♭5 C5 D5
G
D E♭ D
Bass 2
Bass Fig. 1
Bass 1
End Bass Fig. 1

Bass 1: w/ Bass Fig. 1 (3 times)
E♭
D
Bass 3
f
Bass 2
D7
E♭maj7
D7
Bass 4 (elec.)
f
Bass 3
Bass 2

D
E♭
D
T
T
T
T
T
17 19 19 19 19 19 19 19
19 20 20 20 20 17 19
12 14 14 14 14 14 14 14
14 15 15 15 15 15 15 14
T
P
14 16 16 16 16 16 16 16
16 17 17 17 17 16
0
H
Basses 3 & 4 tacet
Bass 2 tacet
D5 N.C.
E♭5 N.C.
E♭5 D5 N.C.
D5 N.C.
Bass 2
Bass 1
0
1 1 0
5

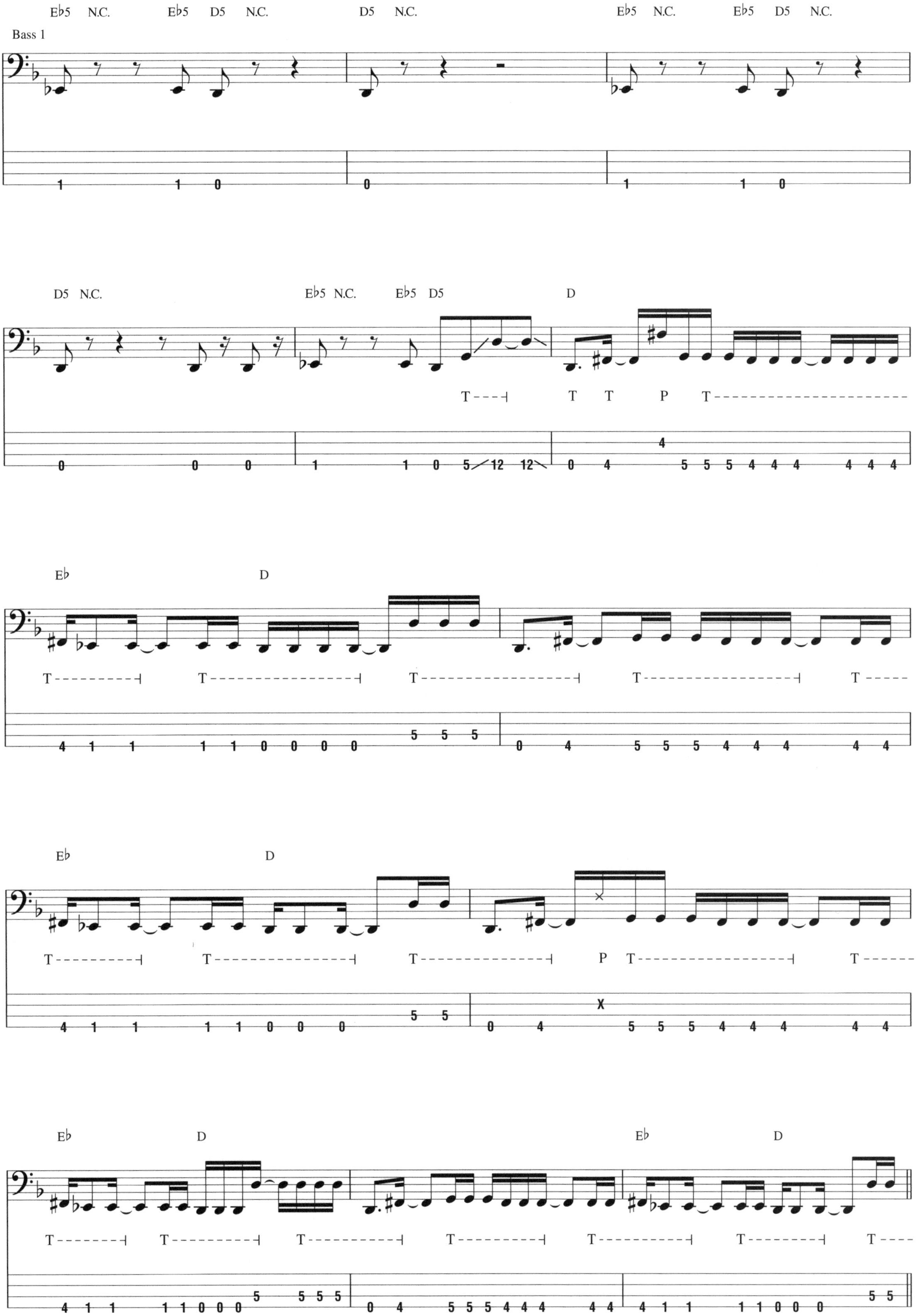
Bass 1
E♭5 N.C. E♭5 D5 N.C. D5 N.C. E♭5 N.C. E♭5 D5 N.C.
D5 N.C. E♭5 N.C. E♭5 D5 D
E♭ D
E♭ D
E♭ D E♭ D

*Guitar Solo arr. for 5-string Tenor Bass. Pitches sound as written.

E♭5
D5
8va
D
loco
E♭
D
E♭
D

E♭
D
8va
loco
E♭
D
8va
J
Bass 5 tacet
D
E♭
D
Bass 1
E♭
D

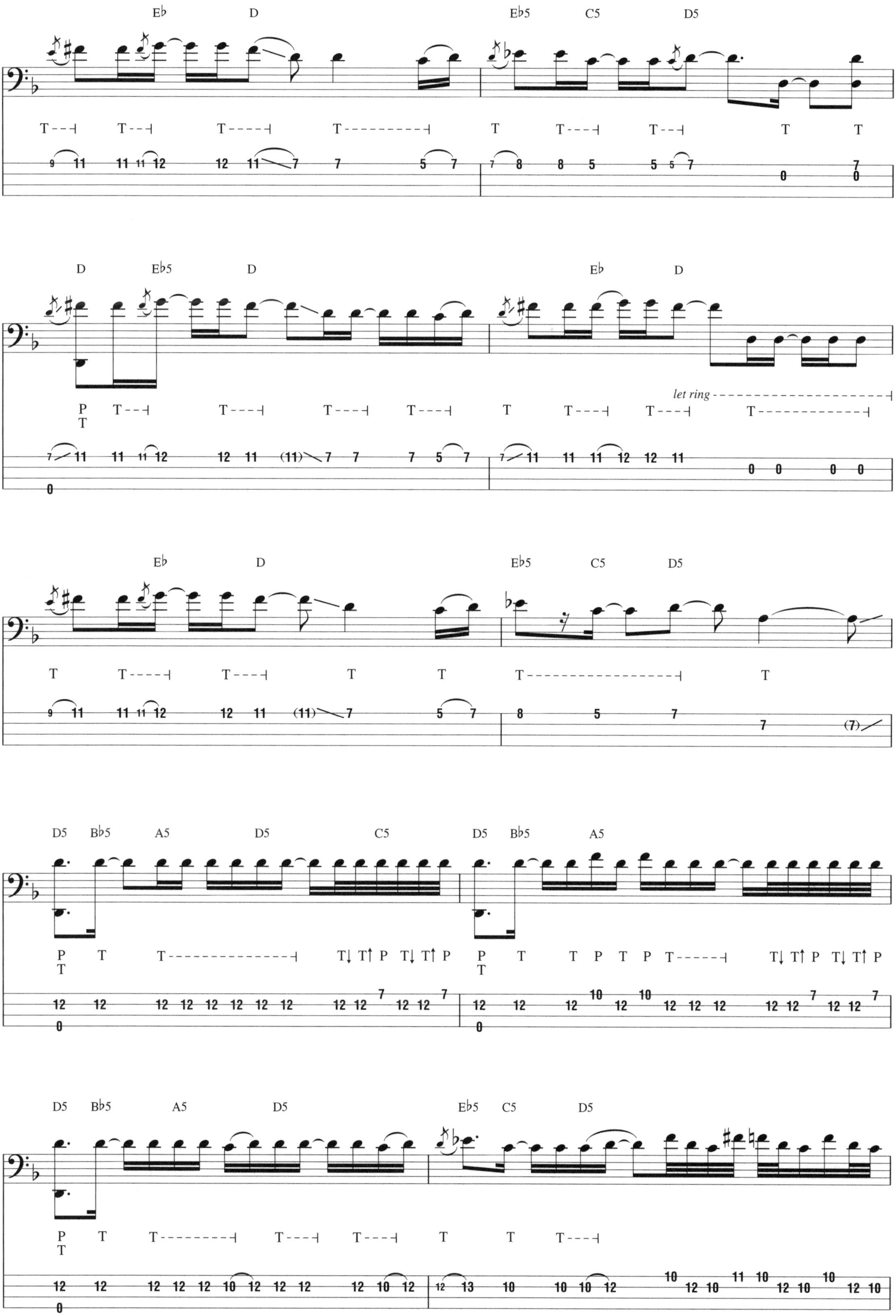
E♭ D
E♭5 C5 D5
D E♭5 D
E♭ D
let ring
E♭ D
E♭5 C5 D5
D5 B♭5 A5 D5 C5
D5 B♭5 A5
D5 B♭5 A5 D5
E♭5 C5 D5

B♭5 A5 D5 C5 D5 B♭5 A5
D5 B♭5 A5 D5 E♭5 C5 D5
Bass 2
Bass 1
E♭ Cm D E♭ Cm D
Bass 3
8va
Bass 2
Bass 1

Basses 2 & 3 tacet
E♭ Cm D
D Dsus4 D N.C.
8va
let ring
steady gliss.
K
D5
Bass 1

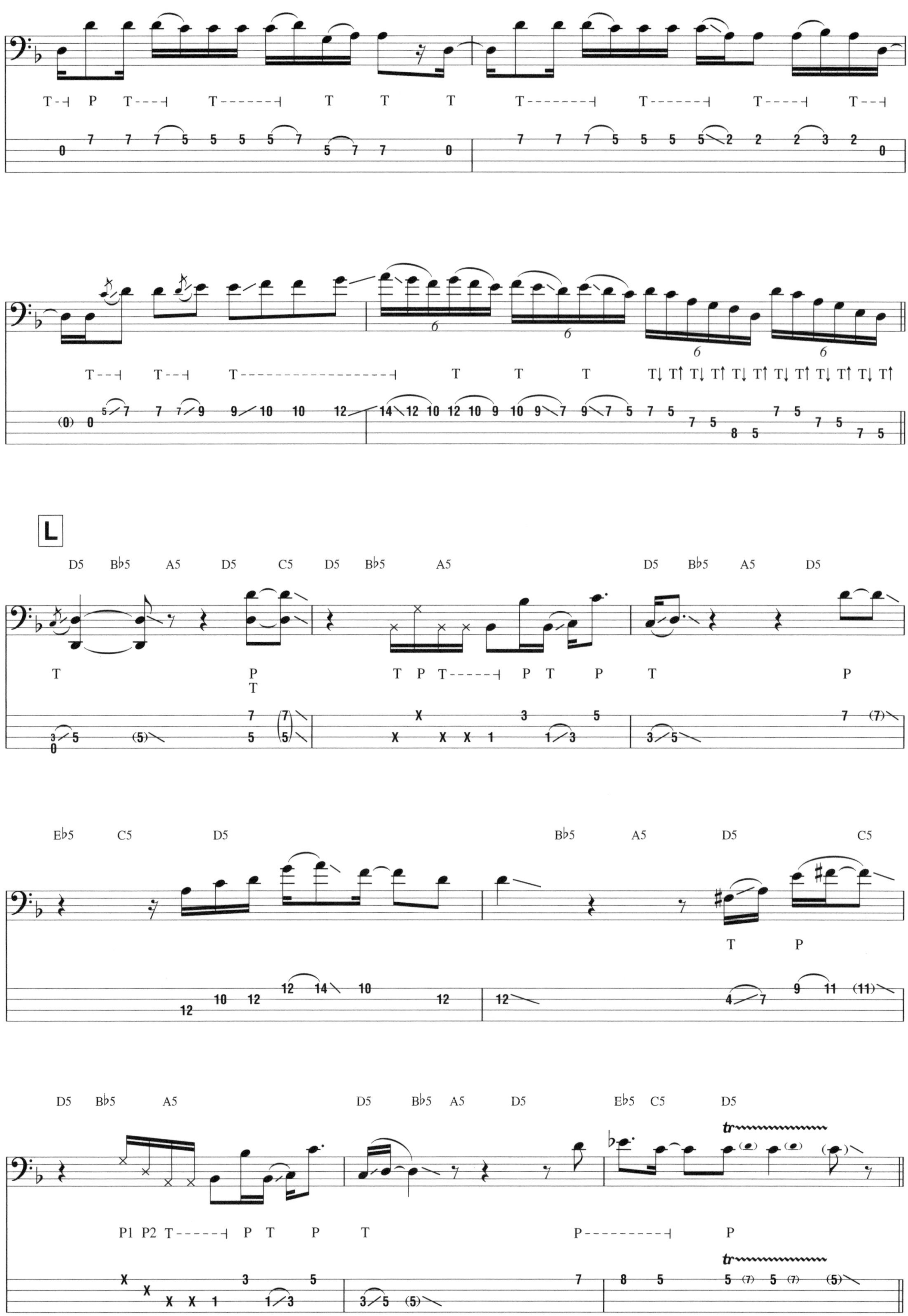
L
D5 B♭5 A5 D5 C5 D5 B♭5 A5 D5 B♭5 A5 D5
E♭5 C5 D5 B♭5 A5 D5 C5
D5 B♭5 A5 D5 B♭5 A5 D5 E♭5 C5 D5
tr

M
D Dsus4 D
Dsus4 D
*T
*w/ T till end
Dsus4 D
E♭5 C5 D5
Bass 1
E♭5 C5 D5
E♭ Cm D
Bass 2
E♭ Cm D
Bass 2 tacet
N.C.
T↓ T↑ P T↓ T↑ P T↓ T↑ P
T↓ T↑ P T↓ T↑ P T↓ T↑ P T↓ T↑ P
tr

from M^2

Boomerang

Words and Music by Marcus Miller

Intro
Moderate Swing ♩ = 123
w/ ad lib. vocals
Bass 1 tacet
B♭m9
Fm7
A♭m9
Bass Fig. 1
*Bass 2
mf
*Sampled acoustic bass.
Bass 1
E♭m9
Bass 2: w/ Bass Fig. 1
B♭m9
Bass 2
End Bass Fig. 1
Fm7
A♭m9
E♭m9
Bass 1
Bass Melody
Bass 2: w/ Bass Fig. 1 (2 times)
B♭m9
Fm7

A♭m9
E♭m9
P P P P T T P
1/2
B♭m9
Fm7
P P P P P P P
A♭m9
E♭m9
1. You're a
P P T T T T↓ T↑ T↓ T↑
1/2
Verse
Bass 2: w/ Bass Fig. 1 (2 times)
B♭m9
Fm7
tak - er, ba - by, tak - in' but nev - er giv - in'. You bet - ter be
T

A♭m9
E♭m9
care - ful, ba - by, ooh, 'bout how you liv - in'. So
B♭m9
Fm7
love don't lie when you break hearts like that.
(Just like a
A♭m9
E♭m9
Just like a boom-er - ang, it's gon - na come right back. Oh,
boom - er - ang.)
Bass Melody
Bass 2: w/ Bass Fig. 1
B♭m9
Fm7
oh.
(Just like a

A♭m9
E♭m9
boom - er - ang.
Just like a boom-er - ang.
2. Now
P P P P T T P T
Verse
Bass 2: w/ Bass Fig. 1 (2 times)
B♭m9
Fm7
when you get through stompin' on my heart like that,
keep your
T
P
A♭m9
E♭m9
eyes o - pen, babe. Ooh, you bet - ter watch your back.
See,
T T T
B♭m9
Fm7
love will turn a - round and do the same damn thing to you.
(Just like a
T
T T

A♭m9
E♭m9
Just like a boom-er - ang, it's gon-na come back to you. Oh, ho, ho.
boom - er - ang.)
T T T T
Bridge
F7sus4
E♭7sus4
B♭m9
Know I love you, babe.
Voc. Fig. 1
(Oh, oh, oh.
Bass 1
P
Bass 2
Bass Fig. 2
F7sus4
E♭7sus4
Cm7
You kept me hang-in' on a string.
Oh, oh, oh.

F7sus4
E♭7sus4
C♭maj7♯11
Oh, ooh, tear out my heart and
Oh, oh, oh.)
End Bass Fig. 2
Bass Fig. 3
C♭
F7♯9
throw it down so what goes a - round comes a - round.
End Voc. Fig. 1
(When ya live,
P
6⁄8
End Bass Fig. 3
Bass Fig. 4
End Bass Fig. 4

Chorus
Bass 2: w/ Bass Fig. 1 (2 times)
B♭m9
Fm7
When you live like that,
live like that,
it's gon - na
Bass 1
A♭m9
E♭m9
don't you know it's gon - na come right back? Oh.
come right back.)
(When you
1/2
B♭m9
Fm7
When you hurt me like you do.
(Just like a
live like that,
when you hurt me like you do.)

A♭m9
E♭m9
Just like a boom-er - ang, it's gon - na come back to you. Yeah.
boom - er - ang.)
Bass Solo
Bass 2: w/ Bass Fig. 1 (2 times)
B♭m9
Fm7
A♭m9
E♭m9
*Played behind the beat.
B♭m9
Lis - ten to what I'm say - in'.

Fm7
A♭m9
Just like a boom - er - ang.
T P P T
10 11 10 8 10 8 10 11 10 8 6 8 6 6 8 8 6
E♭m9
P + + +
6 8 6 0 6 8 13 8 6 0 6 8 13 8 6 0 6 8 15 13 15 13 15
13 13 15 15 13 11 13 11
Bridge
Bkgd. voc.: w/ Voc. Fig. 1
Bass 2: w/ Bass Fig. 2
F7sus4
E♭7sus4
B♭m9
You know I love you, babe.
13 (13)
6 8 6 8 6 8 6 8
F7sus4
E♭7sus4
Cm7
You kept me hang - in' on a string.
8 10 8 10 6 (10) 6 8 6 6

Bass 2: w/ Bass Fig. 3 (3 times)
F7sus4
E♭7sus4
C♭maj7♯11
Oh.
Tear out my heart and throw it down,
6 8 (8)
13 15
13 15
stomp my feel - ings on the ground. I'll be all right. Can't
(Ah, ah,
13 15 13
13 13 15 (15)
14
Bass 2: w/ Bass Fig. 4
F7♯9
keep me down. What goes a - round comes a - round.
ah.)
13 13 15
13 15 13
15 20

Bass 2: w/ Bass Fig. 1 (2 times)
B♭m9
Fm7
When you live like that, (It's gon - na
(Live like that.)
P P P P T P
A♭m9
E♭m9
don't you know it's gon - na come right back? Oh,
come right back.)
P P P 1/2 P P T
B♭m9
ho, ho. When you hurt me
(And when you live like that.)
P P P P
Fm7
A♭m9
like you do. Just like a, just like a
(Just like a boom - er - ang.)
P P T P T T T

E♭m9
boom - er - ang.
It's gon - na come back to you.
Yeah.
Trumpet Solo
B♭m
8va
loco

E♭m7
E°7
F7
(When you
Verse
Bass 2: w/ Bass Fig. 1 (2 times)
B♭m9
Fm7
live like that.)
3. Ooh, when you take but nev - er give, ba - by.
(It's gon - na
A♭m9
E♭m9
come right back.)
Bet - ter check out how you're liv - in', babe.
Like you're liv - in', liv - in', ba - by.
(And when you
B♭m9
Fm7
When you hurt me like you do.
live like that.)
(Just like a

A♭m9
E♭m9
Just like a boomer - ang.
boom - er - ang.)
Outro
Bass 2: w/ Bass Fig. 1 (4 times)
B♭m9
Fm7
*Played behind the beat.
A♭m9
E♭m9
B♭m9
Fm7
A♭m9

E♭m9
B♭m9
Ain't no back and forth.
Fm7
A♭m9
E♭m9
B♭m9
Fm7
A♭m9
E♭m9

from *Silver Rain*

Bruce Lee

By Marcus Miller

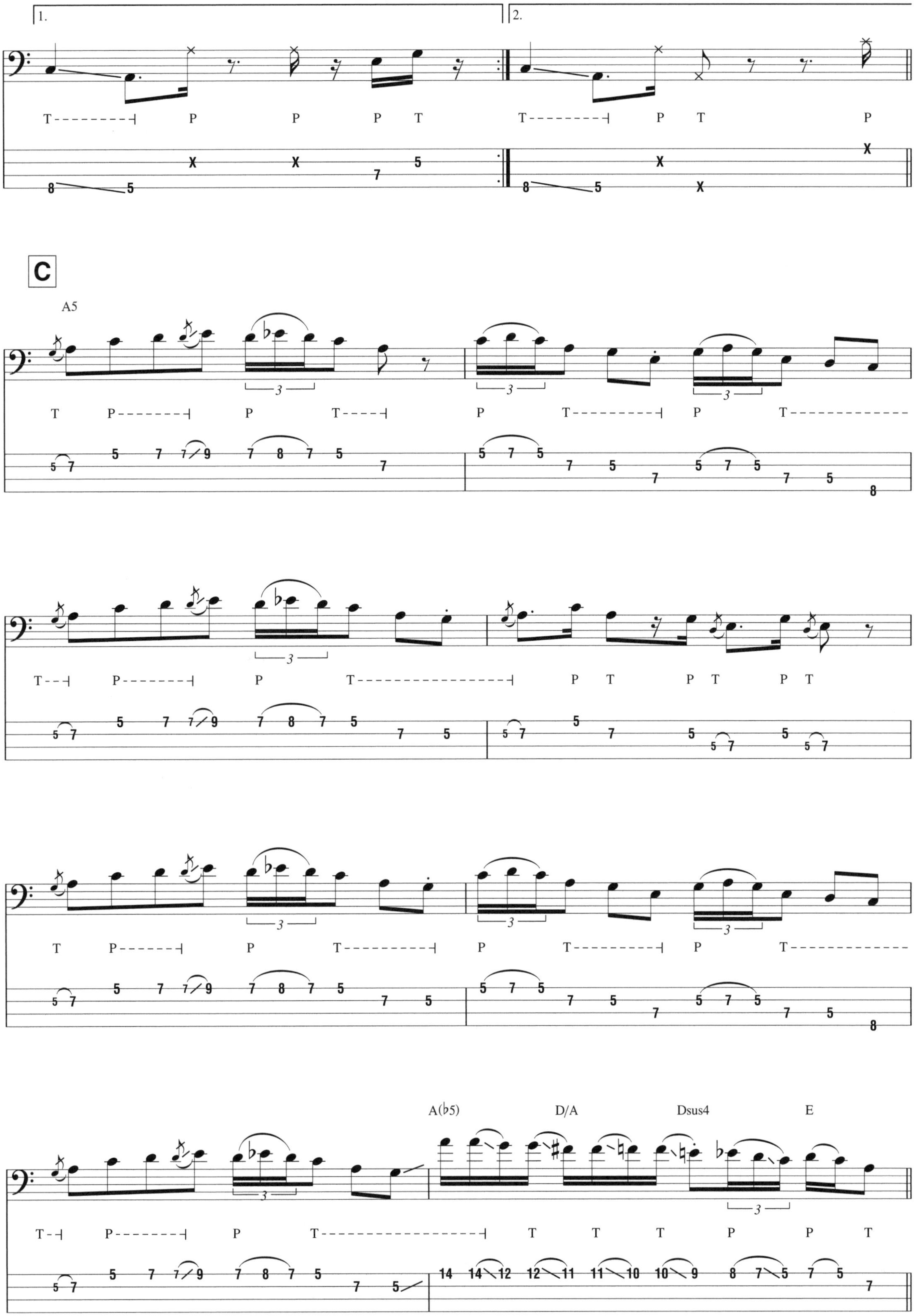
1.
2.
C
A5
A(♭5)
D/A
Dsus4
E

D
A5
1/4
E
A5
A(♭5)
D/A
Dsus4
E

F

A5

G

A5

*Rake w/ fingertips.

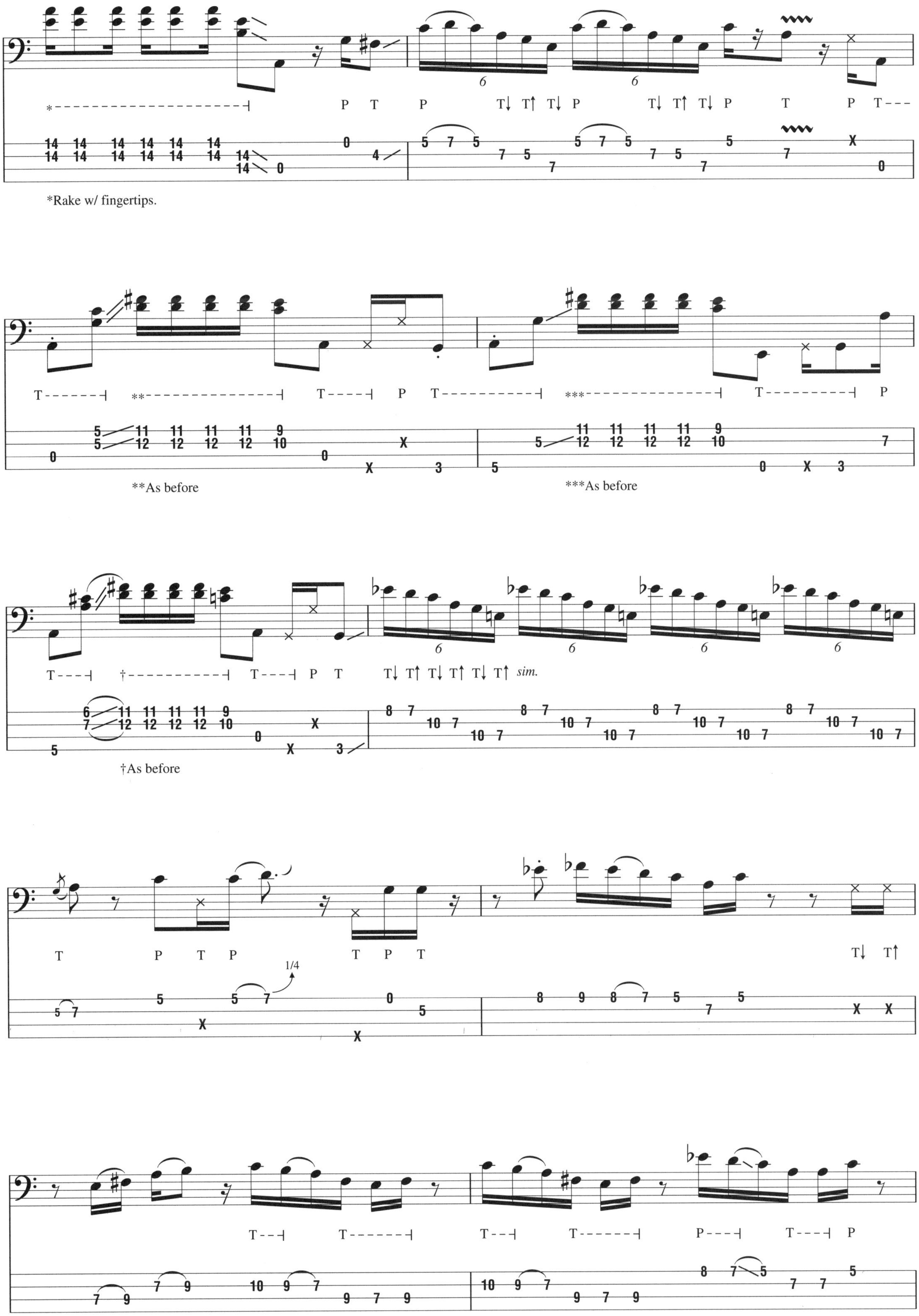
*Rake w/ fingertips.
**As before
***As before
sim.
†As before
1/4

I
A5
J
A5

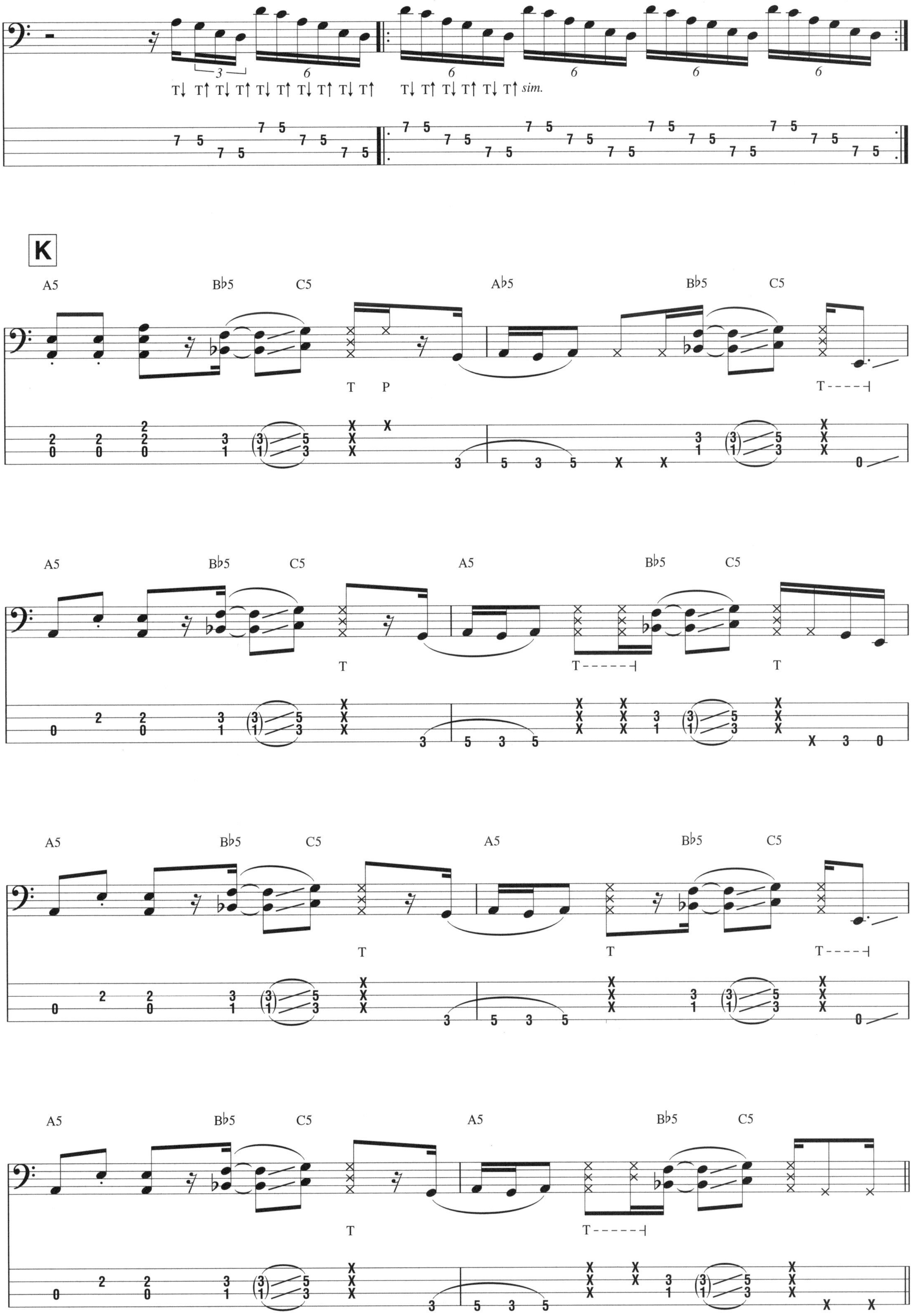
sim.
K
A5 B♭5 C5 A♭5 B♭5 C5
T P T
A5 B♭5 C5 A5 B♭5 C5
T T T
A5 B♭5 C5 A5 B♭5 C5
T T T
A5 B♭5 C5 A5 B♭5 C5
T T

L
A5 B♭5 C5 A5 B♭5 C5
A5 B♭5 C5 A5 B♭5 C5
A5 B♭5 C5 A5 B♭5 C5
A5 B♭5 C5 A5 B♭5 C5
T
A5 B♭5 C5 A5 B♭5 C5

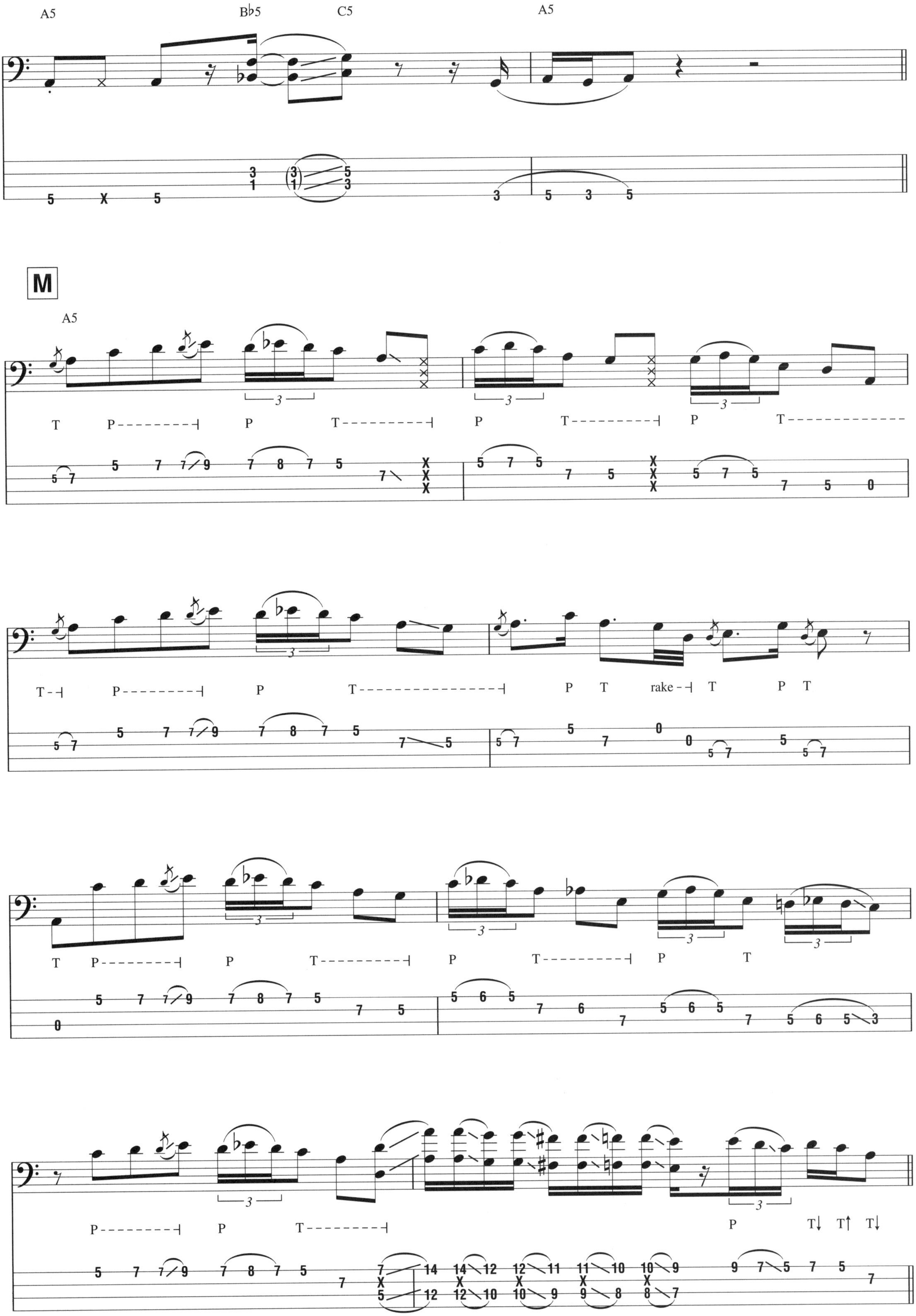
A5
B♭5
C5
A5
M
A5
T
P
rake

N
A5
1/2
1/2
tr
tr

from *Suddenly*

Could It Be You

By Marcus Miller

C
♩= 74
Bmaj7
A♭m7
B♭sus4
B♭7
8va
loco
D♭7sus4
C7♭5
G♭7
Bmaj7
F7
D
B♭maj7
Dm7
C7
E♭7♯11
Dm7
G7♯9
E
A♭7sus4
D♭maj9
D♭maj7
C7♭13
G♭11
Bmaj9
G♭11
mp
mf
F
Bmaj7
A♭m7
F11
B♭sus4

G
♩ = 76
Ebm7
Ab7#9
A11
D9
D9b5
8va
loco
D7sus4

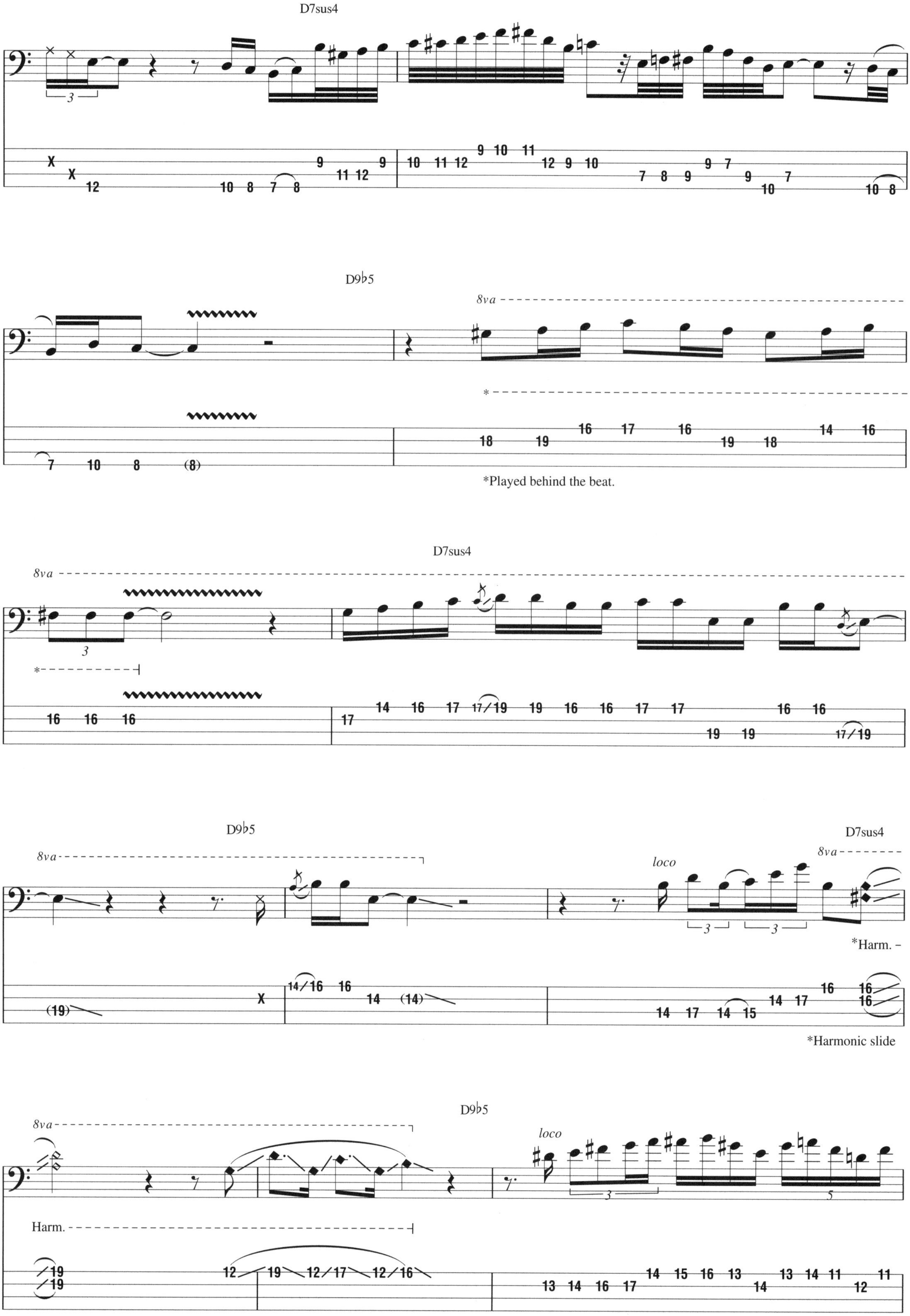
D7sus4
D9♭5
8va
*Played behind the beat.
D7sus4
8va
D9♭5
8va
loco
D7sus4
8va
*Harm.
*Harmonic slide
8va
Harm.
D9♭5
loco

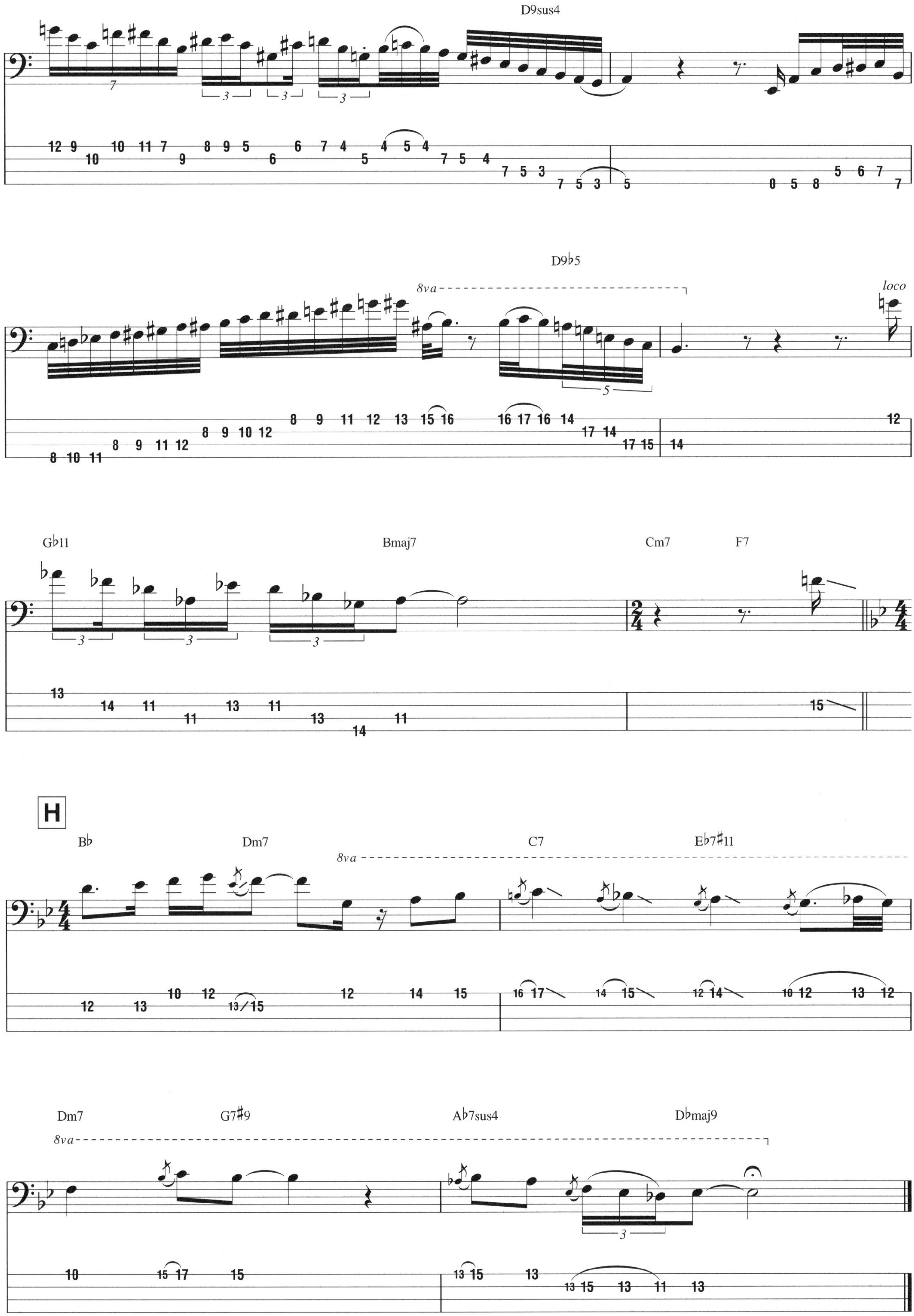
D9sus4
D9♭5
8va
loco
G♭11
Bmaj7
Cm7
F7
H
B♭
Dm7
C7
E♭7♯11
Dm7
G7♯9
A♭7sus4
D♭maj9

from *Tales*

Ethiopia

By Marcus Miller

E7sus4
Am13
Ebm7
F13(add4)
B7b9
E7sus4
Am13
E6
Bm6/9
E7sus4
Am13

E♭m7
F13(add4)
B7♭9
8va
C
Em
loco
T P T P
P
T
P T T
E7sus4
T P T P T
Am13
E6
Dm6/9
P T

E♭m7
F13(add4)
B7♭9
T P T
P T P T P
D
Em
8va
B7♭9
loco
T
E
E7sus4
Am13
T
T P T P T
P

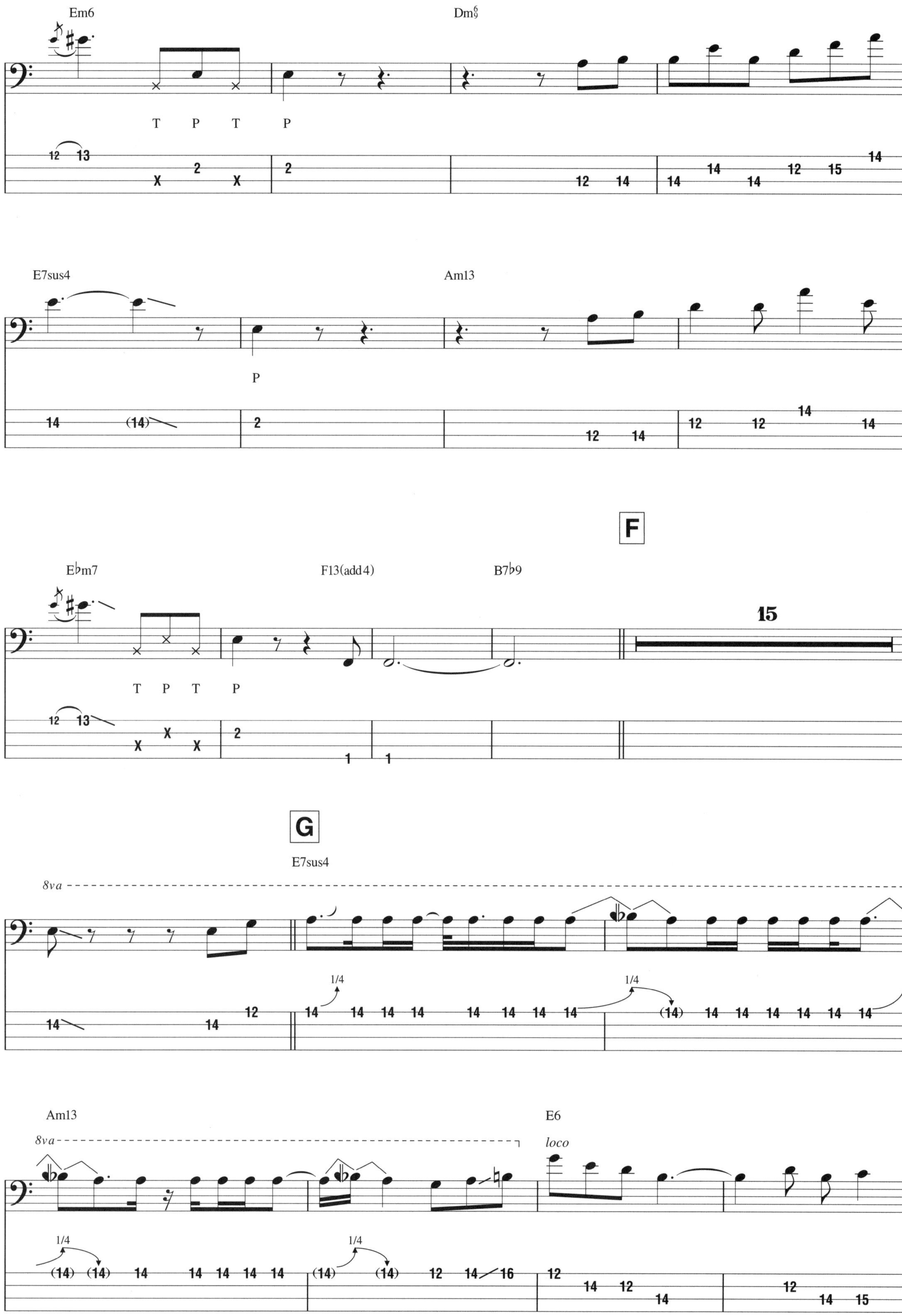
Em6
Dm6/9
T P T P
E7sus4
Am13
P
F
Ebm7
F13(add4)
B7b9
15
T P T P
G
E7sus4
8va
1/4
Am13
8va
E6
loco
1/4

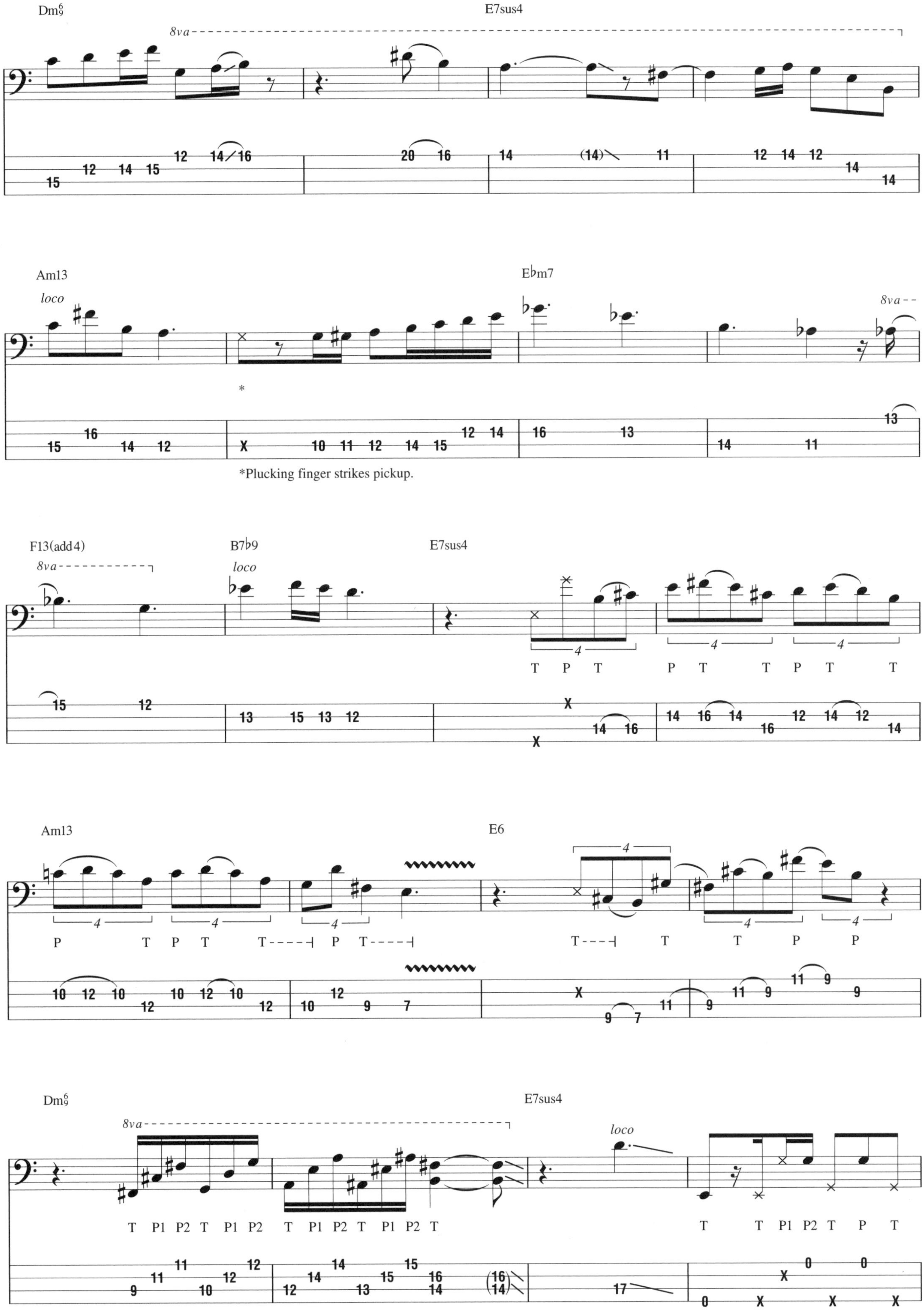
Dm⁶₉
E7sus4
8va
Am13
loco
E♭m7
8va
*Plucking finger strikes pickup.
F13(add4)
8va
B7♭9
loco
E7sus4
T P T
P T T P T T
Am13
P T P T T P T
E6
T T T P P
Dm⁶₉
8va
T P1 P2 T P1 P2 T P1 P2 T P1 P2 T
E7sus4
loco
T T P1 P2 T P T

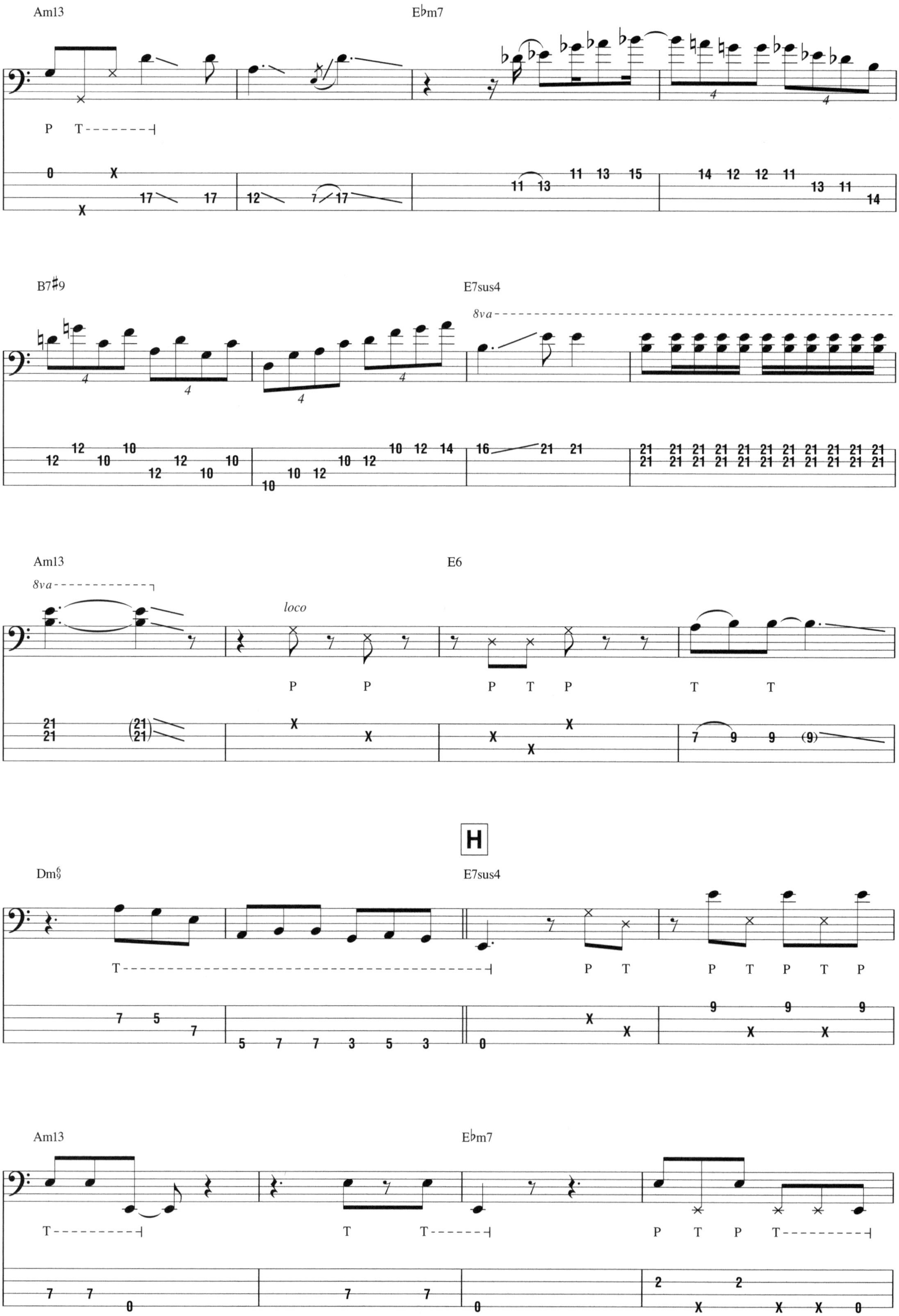
Am13
E♭m7
B7♯9
E7sus4
8va
Am13
8va
loco
E6
H
Dm6/9
E7sus4
Am13
E♭m7

*Played ahead of the beat.

8va
8va
loco
J
E7sus4
Am13
E6
Dm6/9
E7sus4

Am13
E♭m7
F13(add4)
K
B7♭9
N.C.
8va

L
E7sus4
Am13
8va
loco
E6
Dm6/9
E7sus4
Am13
E♭m7
F13(add4)
B7♭9
E7sus4
Am13
steady gliss.
E6
Dm6/9

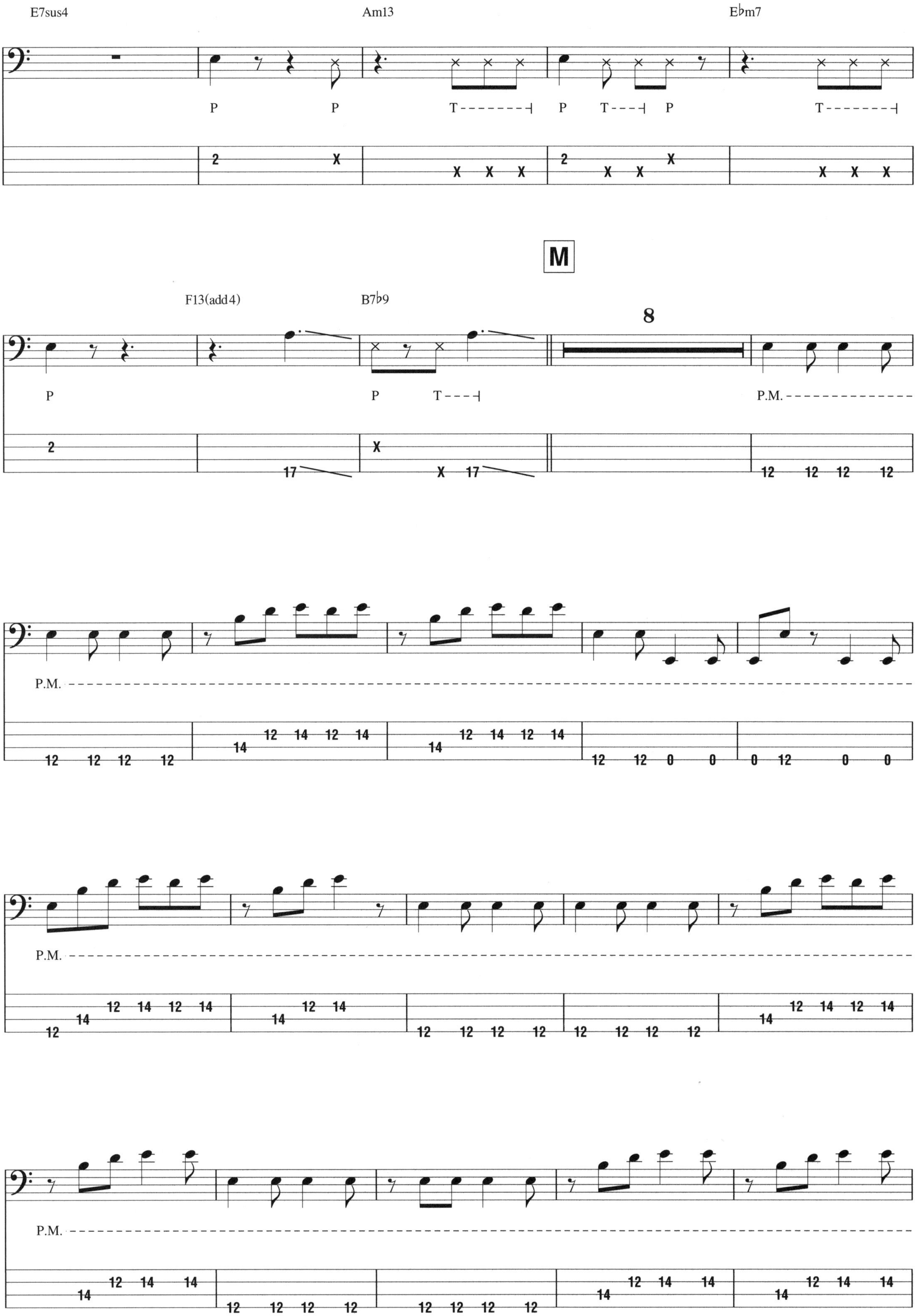
E7sus4
Am13
E♭m7
M
F13(add4)
B7♭9
8
P
T
P.M.

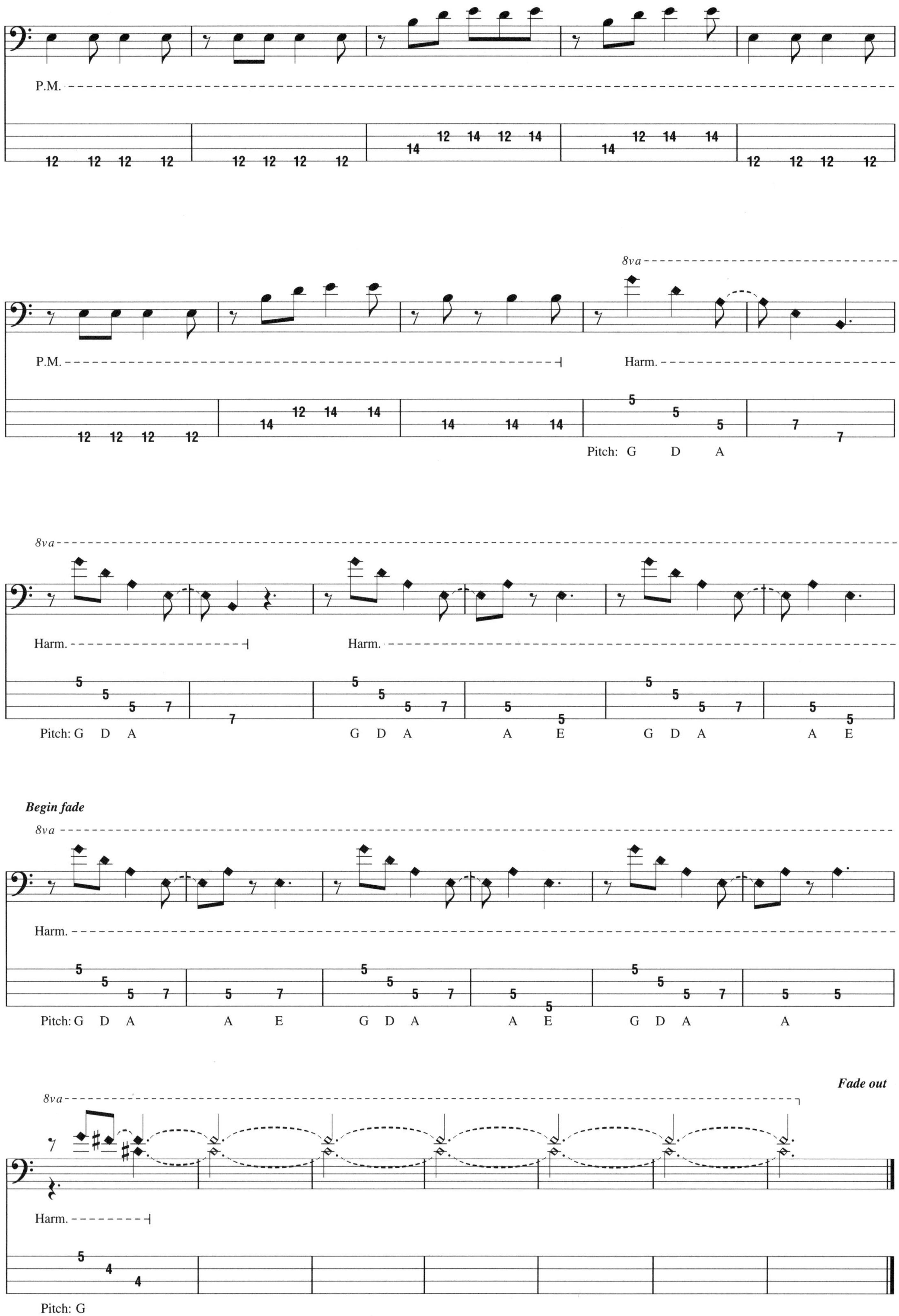
P.M.
P.M.
8va
Harm.
Pitch: G D A
8va
Harm.
Harm.
Pitch: G D A
G D A
A E
G D A
A E
Begin fade
8va
Harm.
Pitch: G D A
A E
G D A
A E
G D A
A
Fade out
8va
Harm.
Pitch: G

from *Tales*

Forevermore

By Marcus Miller

C
G
F♯m7
Bm7
Em9
8va
G
F♯m7 Bm7
Em9
loco
A11
8va
Am13
D7
8va
Gmaj7
D/F♯
loco
E
A11
Dsus4
D
8va
D
Bm
Gmaj7/B
Amaj7/B
8va

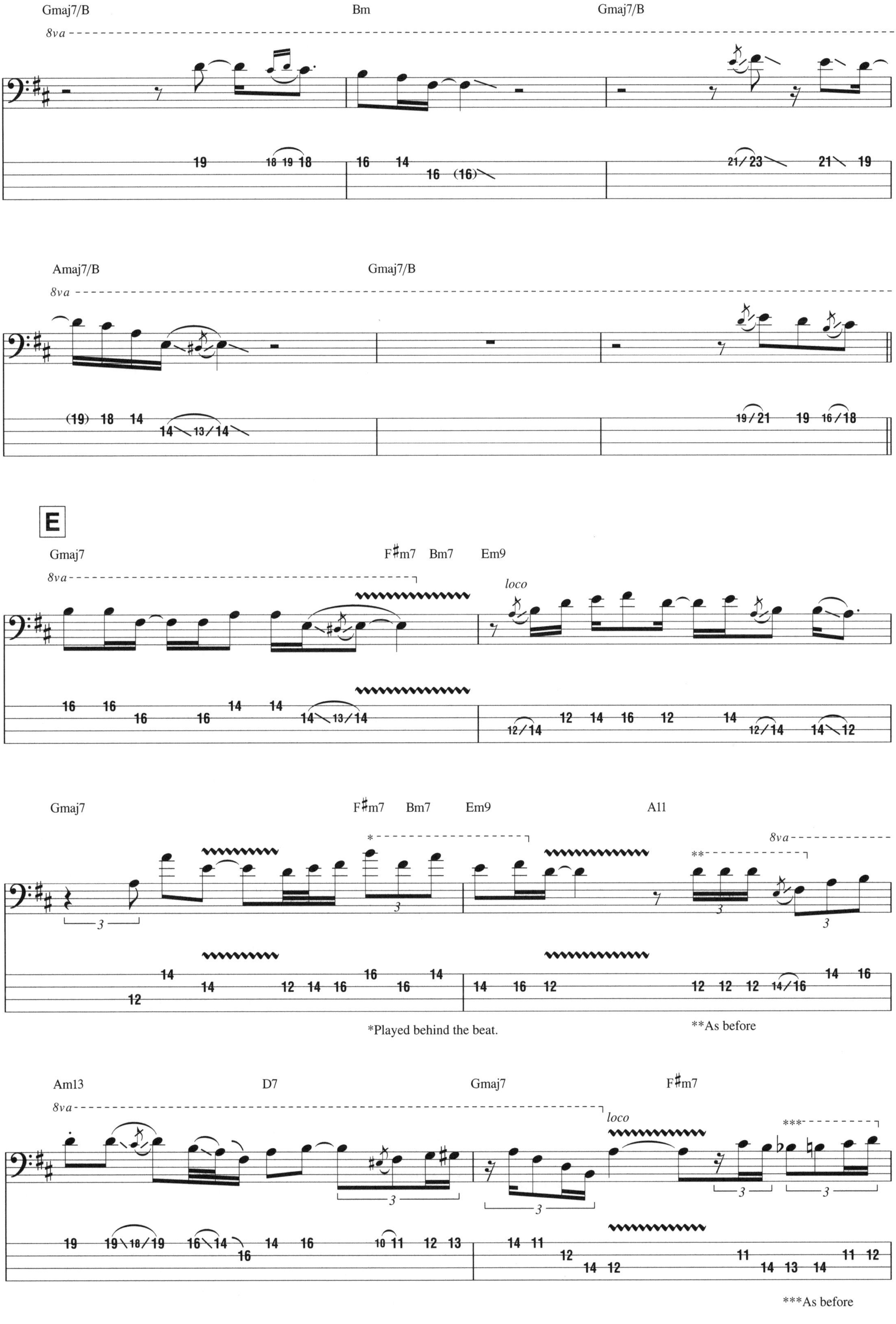
Gmaj7/B
Bm
Gmaj7/B
8va
Amaj7/B
Gmaj7/B
8va
E
Gmaj7
F♯m7
Bm7
Em9
8va
loco
Gmaj7
F♯m7
Bm7
Em9
A11
8va
*Played behind the beat.
**As before
Am13
D7
Gmaj7
F♯m7
8va
loco
***As before

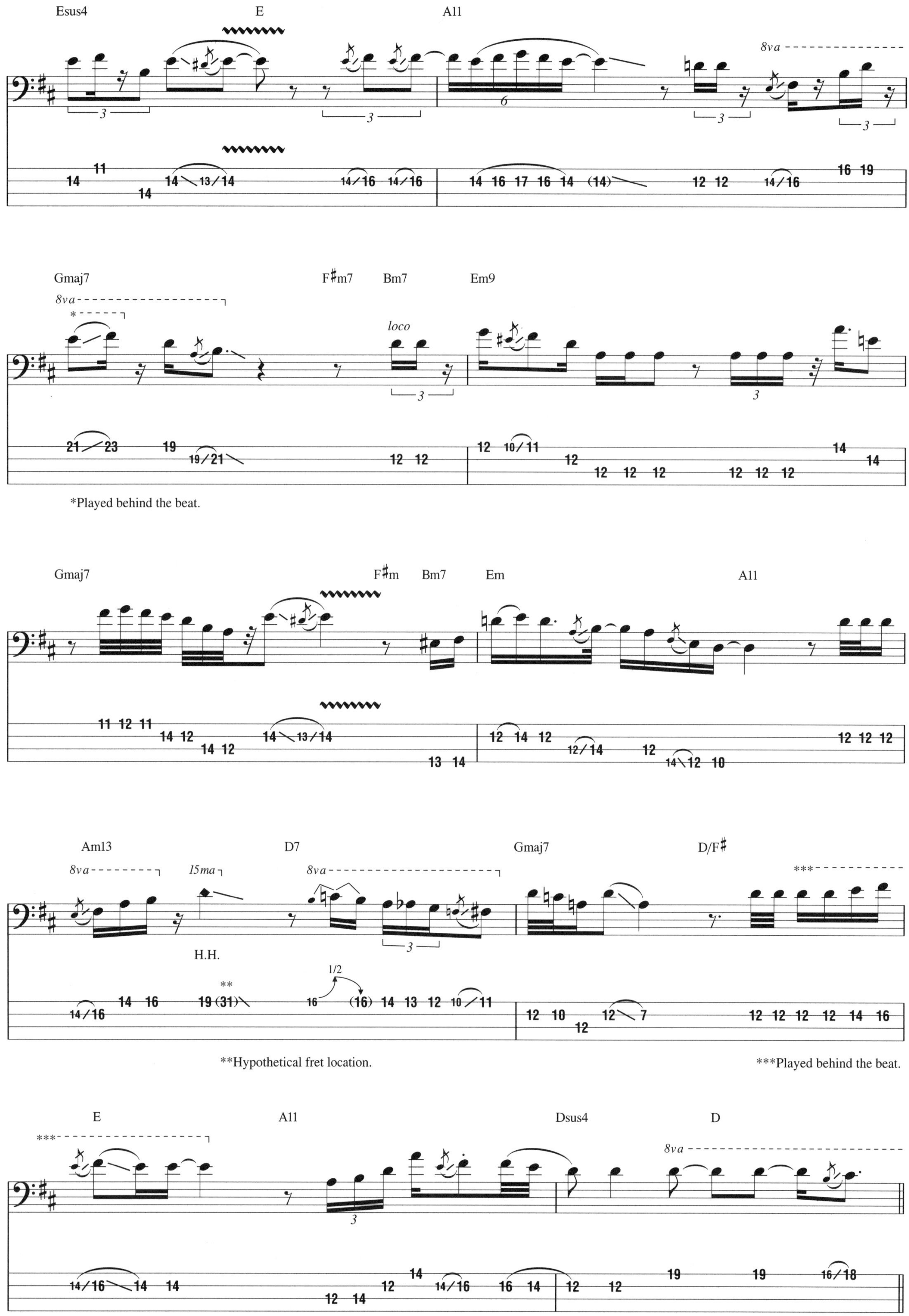
Esus4
E
A11
8va
Gmaj7
F♯m7
Bm7
Em9
loco
*Played behind the beat.
Gmaj7
F♯m
Bm7
Em
A11
Am13
D7
Gmaj7
D/F♯
15ma
H.H.
1/2
**Hypothetical fret location.
***Played behind the beat.
E
A11
Dsus4
D

*Played behind the beat.

Gmaj7/B
8va
G
Freely ♩ = 65
Gmaj7
F♯m7
Bm7
Em9
Gmaj7
F♯m7
Bm7
8va
Em9
A11
Am13
D7
Gmaj7
D/F♯
loco
8va
loco
E
A11
Bsus4
B
E
A
*Played behind the beat.
Dsus4
D
E6
A11
8va
loco

H
♩. = 70
B♭
8va
9
G
E
C
E
A11
loco
Dsus4
D
Harm.
Pitch: D A E

from *The Sun Don't Lie*

Funny

By Marcus Miller and Boz Scaggs

C♭/D♭
Amaj7♯11/C♯
1.
Bass 2
tr
P
tr
Bass 1
8vb
End Bass Fig. 2
2.
Bass 1: w/ Bass Fig. 1 (2 times)
Bass 2
tr
8va
loco
P
tr
1/4
1/4
C
D11
F11
F11♭5
Bass 2
T
T
Bass 1

C6/9
D♭maj7
Dm7
Gm7
G♭maj7♯11
Fsus4
F7♯9
F7♭9
To Coda
8va
D
Bass 1: w/ Bass Fig. 2
B♭5
C♭/B♭
B♭sus2
C♭/D♭
Amaj7♯11/C♯
All she needs is love.
Bass 2
loco
C♭/D♭
Amaj7♯11/C♯

B♭5
E
Bass 1: w/ Bass Fig. 1 (4 times)
B♭5
F
Bass 1: w/ Bass Fig. 2 (2 times)
B♭5
C♭/B♭
B♭sus2
C♭/D♭
Amaj7♯11/C♯

Cb/Db Amaj7#11/C#
Bb5
Bb5
8va
Cb/Bb Bbsus2
loco
Cb/Db Amaj7#11/C#
Cb/Db Amaj7#11/C#
Bb5
Ab5 Bb5

D.S. al Coda
Ab5
Bb5
8va
loco
P
Coda
G
Bass 1: w/ Bass Fig. 2
Bb5
C/Bb
Bbsus2
Cb/Db
Amaj7#11/C#
All she needs is love.
Bass 2
8va
P
loco
T T
Cb/Db
Amaj7#11/C#
P
T P P P T
Bb5
T T
P
8va
loco
P.M.
Bass 2 tacet
Bb5
C6/Bb
Bbsus2
Cb/Db
Amaj7#11/C#
All she needs is love.

Cb/Db
Amaj7#11/C#
Bb5
Bass 2
Ab5 Bb5
Ab5 Bb5
H
Bass 1: w/ Bass Fig. 1 (8 times)
Bb5
So deep in - side.
So deep in - side your love.
So deep in - side your love.
Get deep in - side.
tr
P
T P

So deep in - side your love.
Get deep in - side.
tr
P P P
1/2
So deep in - side your love.
P T T T T P T T
Get deep in - side.
So deep in - side your love.
T P P P
w/ ad lib. vocal (till fade)

I
Bass 1: w/ Bass Fig. 1 (till fade)
B♭5
tr
P
T
P
P
P
T
T
P.M.
Begin fade
tr
P
T
Fade out
3
tr
P P P P T P
P

from *Silver Rain*

La Villette

Words and Music by Marcus Miller and Lalah Hathaway

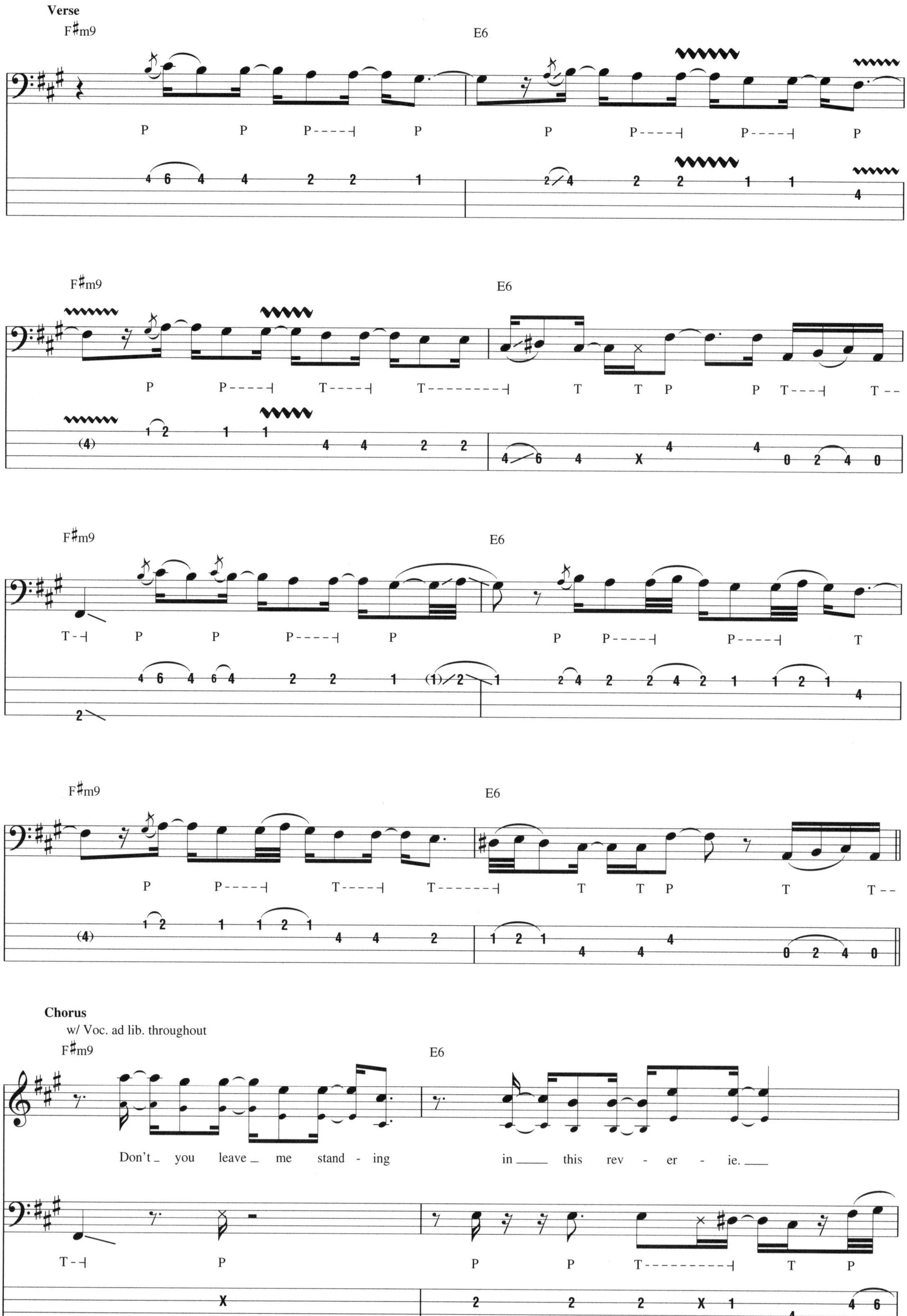
Verse
F#m9
E6
P P P P P P P P
F#m9
E6
P P T T T T P P T T
F#m9
E6
T P P P P P P P T
F#m9
E6
P P T T T T P T T
Chorus
w/ Voc. ad lib. throughout
F#m9
E6
Don't _ you leave _ me stand - ing in ___ this rev - er - ie. ___
T P P P T T P

F♯m9
E6
Hold - ing on to flow - er fad - ed mem - o - ry.
F♯m9
E6
I can hear the laugh - ter of what used to be.
F♯m9
E6
The nights of La Vil - lette will for - ev - er be with me.
Verse
F♯m9
E6

F♯m9
E6
F♯m9
E6
F♯m9
E6
Chorus
F♯m9
E6
Close my eyes and it's just like you're here with me.
F♯m9
E6
Then I re - al - ize it's just my fan - ta - sy.

F♯m9
E6
For you I know it was just nights of ec - sta - sy.
P
T
P P P
4
X
0
2 2 2 2 2
F♯m9
E6
The nights of La Vil - lette will for - ev - er be with me.
P T P P1 P2 T T↓ T↑ T T↓ T↑ T T
1
X 4 4 X X
2 2 2 2 2 2 2 2 2
Bridge
2nd time, Bass: w/ Bass Fill 1
D
B°
D
F♯sus4
F♯maj7
Voc. Fig. 1
Ah.
11

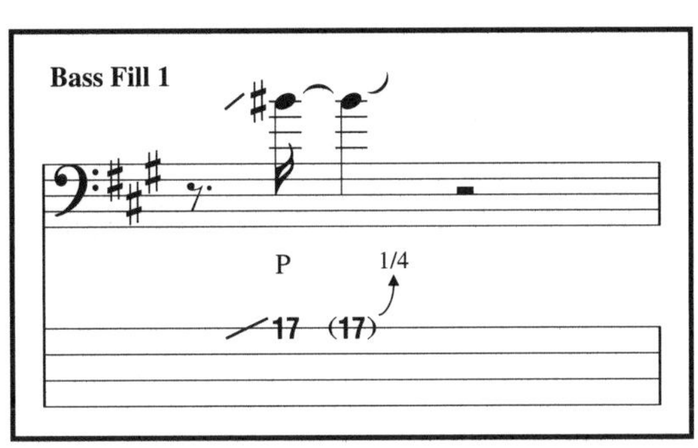
Bass Fill 1
P
1/4
17 (17)

D
B°
End Voc. Fig. 1
Ah.
D
C♯sus4
C♯
F♯m9
E6
To Coda 1
To Coda 2
F♯m9
E6

Bass Solo

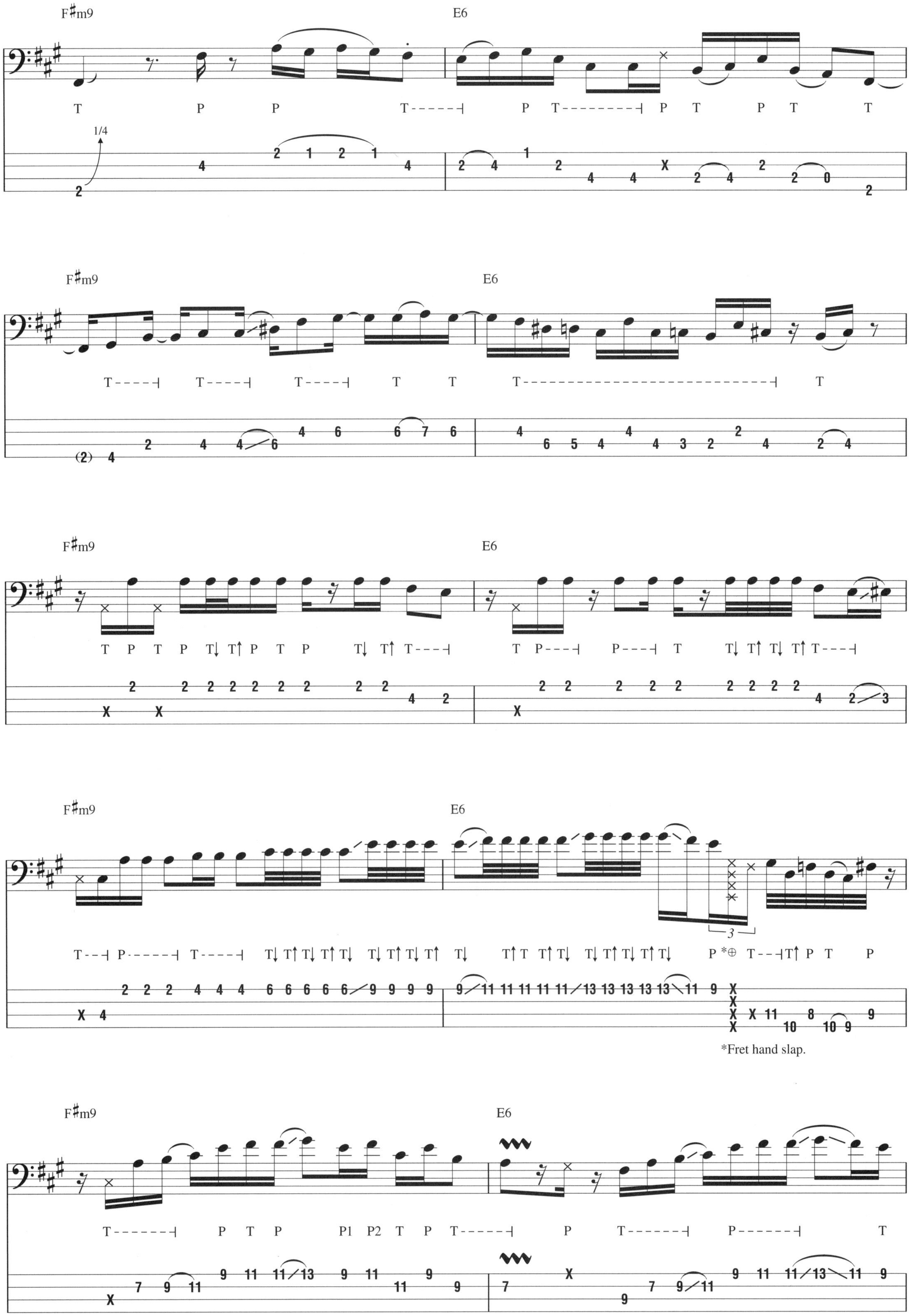

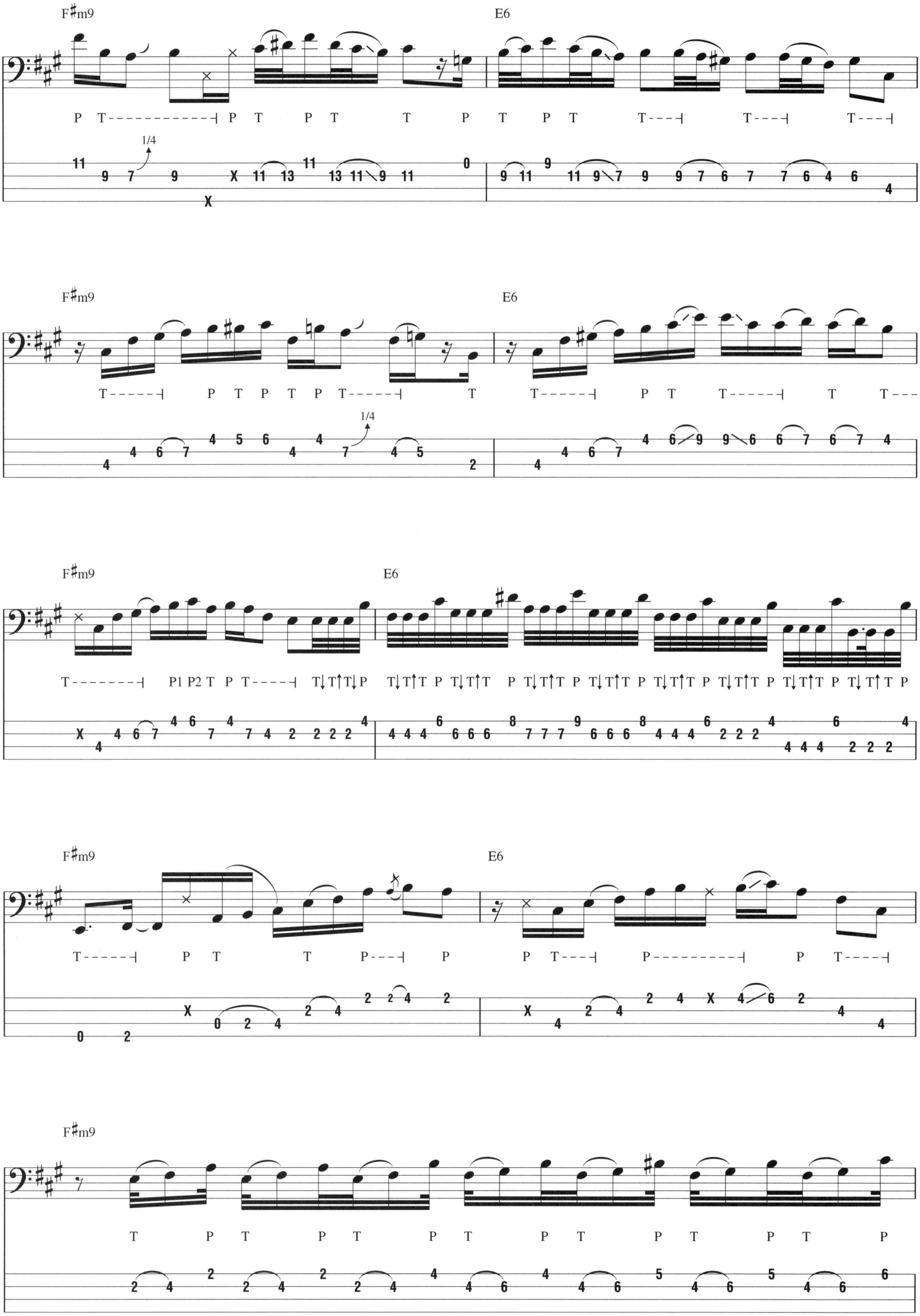
F♯m9
E6
F♯m9
E6
F♯m9
E6
F♯m9
E6
F♯m9

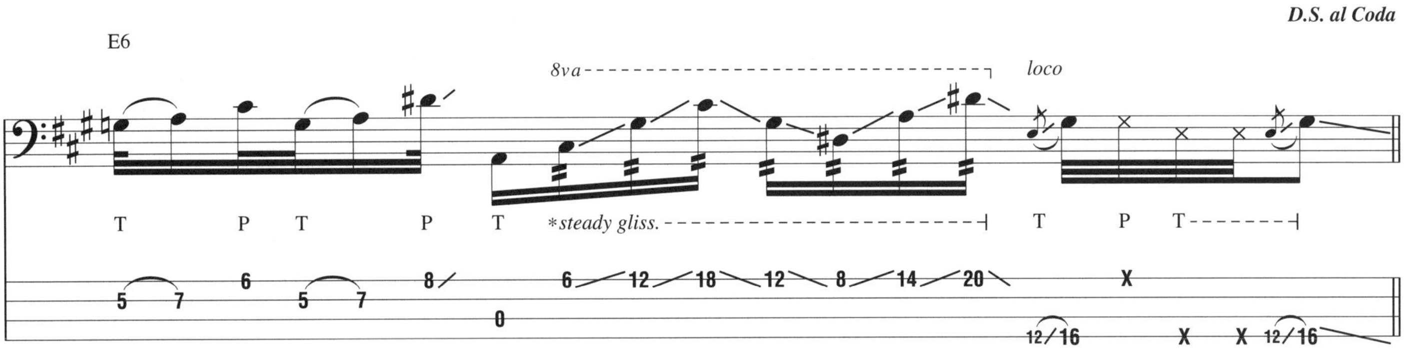

*Using 3 or 4 right-hand fingers, pluck notes as fast as possible while ascending and descending as indicated.

Coda 1

Verse

Chorus
F♯m9
E6
Close _ my eyes _ and it's _ just like _ you're here _ with me. _
F♯m9
E6
Then _ I re - al - ize _ it's just _ my fan - ta - sy. _
F♯m9
E6
For you _ I know _ it was _ just nights _ of ec - sta - sy. _
F♯m9
E6
The nights _ of La _ Vil - lette _ will for - ev - er be _ with me. _

Bridge
Voc.: w/ Voc. Fig. 1
Bass tacet
D
B°
D
F♯sus4
F♯maj7
Bass
C♯sus4
C♯
D.S.S. al Coda
Coda 2
F♯m9
E6
8va

Outro-Chorus
F♯m9
Close my eyes and it's just
8va
E6
like you're here with me.
8va
loco
F♯m9
E6
Then I re-al-ize it's just my fan-ta-sy.
Bass tacet
F♯m9
E6
For you I know it was just nights of ec-sta-sy.
F♯m9
E6
F♯m9
The nights of La Vil-lette will for-ev-er be with me.

from M^2

Lonnie's Lament

By John Coltrane

1., 2.
Cm6
D°7
E♭6
D°7
Bass Fig. 1
End Bass Fig. 1
3.
C
Bass 2 tacet
E♭6
D°7
G7♯9
G♯7♭9
Cm6
D°7
Bass 3
mf
Bass 2
*Bass 2: w/ Bass Fig. 1
E♭6
D°7
Cm6
D°7
E♭6
D°7
Bass 3
*Bass 2 will play variations on recalls.
Cm6
D°7
E♭6
D°7
Bass 2: w/ Bass Fig. 1
Cm6
D°7

D
E♭6 D°7 Cm6 B♭13 E♭maj7 A♭maj7
A♭13 A13 A♭13 G7♯9
E
Bass 2: w/ Bass Fig. 1 (2 times)
Cm6 D°7 E♭6 Gm7 G7 Cm6 D°7
E♭6 Gm7 G7 Cm6 D°7 E♭6 Gm7 G7
T P
F
Cm6 D°7 E♭6 D°7 Cm6 D°7
P.M.
P.M.

E♭6 D°7 Cm6 D°7 E♭6 D°7
Cm6 D°7 E♭6 D°7
G
Cm6 D°7 E♭6 D°7
Cm6 D°7 E♭6 D°7
Cm6 D°7 E♭6 D°7

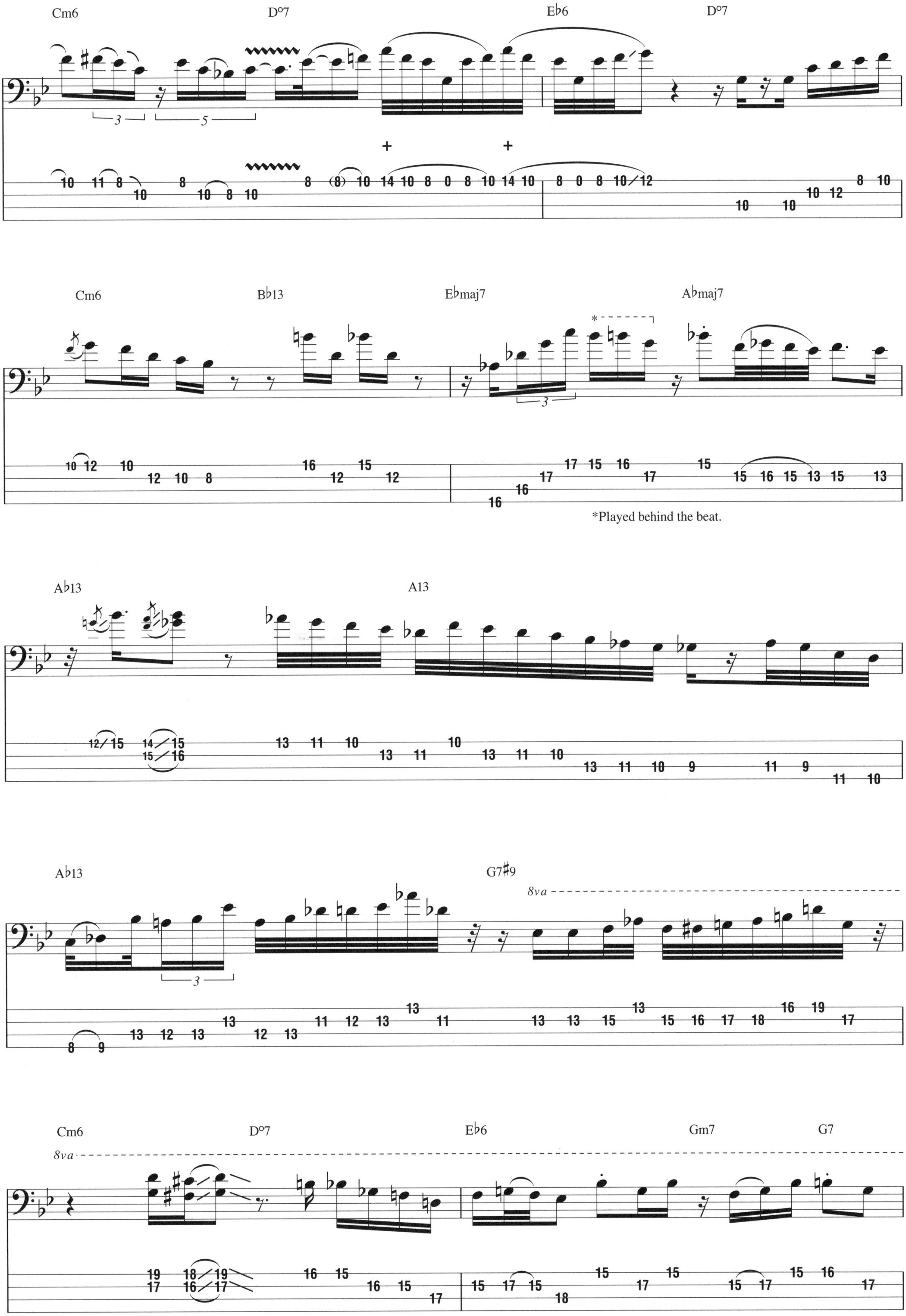
Cm6 D°7 E♭6 D°7
Cm6 B♭13 E♭maj7 A♭maj7
*Played behind the beat.
A♭13 A13
A♭13 G7♯9
8va
Cm6 D°7 E♭6 Gm7 G7
8va

Bass 2: w/ Bass Fig. 1 (1 1/2 times)
Cm6 D°7 E♭6 Gm7 G7
8va
loco
Cm6 D°7 E♭6 Am7 A7
H
Dm6 E°7 F6 E°7 Dm6 E°7
F6 E°7 Dm6 E°7 F6 E°7
Dm6 E°7 F6 Gm7 G7 Cm6 D°7
8va
loco

E♭6 D°7 Cm6 D°7 E♭6 D°7
Cm6 D°7 E♭6 D°7 Cm6 D°7
8va loco
I
E♭6 D°7 Cm6 D°7 E♭6 D°7
tr
Cm6 D°7 E♭6 D°7 Cm6 D°7
tr
E♭6 D°7 Cm6 D°7 E♭6 D°7

J
Cm6
B♭13
E♭maj7
A♭maj7
A♭13
A13
A♭13
G7♯9
Cm6
D°7
E♭6
Gm7
G7
Bass 2: w/ Bass Fig. 1
Cm6
D°7
E♭6
Gm7
G7
Cm6
D°7
E♭6
Gm7
G7
Cm6
D°7
E♭6
Gm7
G7
8va
*Plucked w/ thumb & index finger.
Cm6
D°7
E♭6
D°7
Cm6
D°7
8va
loco
let ring

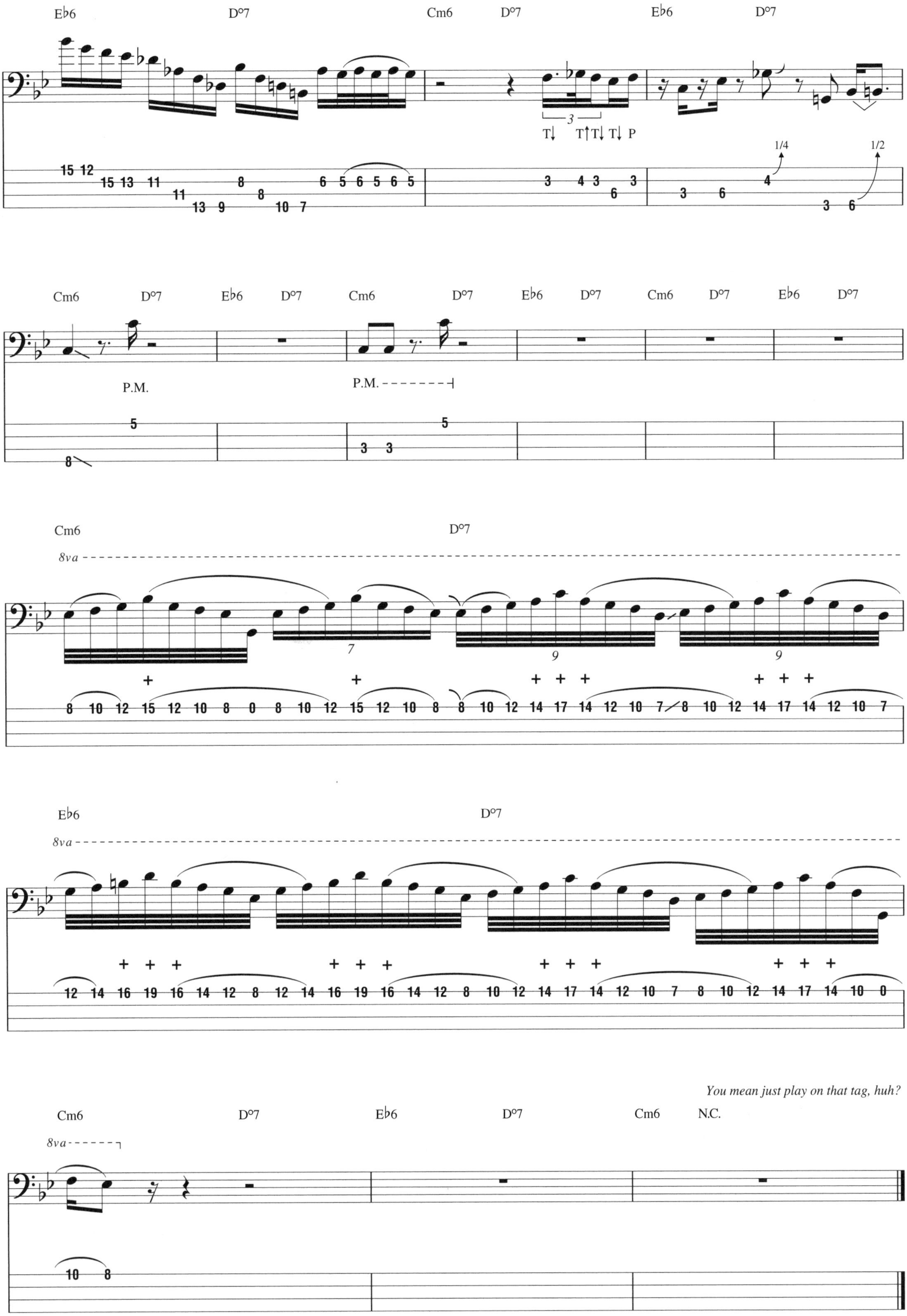
E♭6 D°7 Cm6 D°7 E♭6 D°7
T↓ T↑T↓ T↓ P
1/4
1/2
Cm6 D°7 E♭6 D°7 Cm6 D°7 E♭6 D°7 Cm6 D°7 E♭6 D°7
P.M.
P.M.
Cm6 D°7
8va
E♭6 D°7
8va
You mean just play on that tag, huh?
Cm6 D°7 E♭6 D°7 Cm6 N.C.
8va

from Bob James - *Double Vision*

Maputo

By Marcus Miller

C
Gm
F
E♭maj7
Gm
Cm
Gm
B♭add13
E♭maj7
Gm
Dm7
Gm
D
Fsus4
B♭
F/A
Gm7
Dm
Gm
Fsus4
B♭
F/A
Gm7

Dm
Gm
F
E♭maj7
E
Gm
F
E♭maj7
Gm
C
Gm
B♭7add13
E♭maj7
Gm
Dm7
Gm
Dm7

F
Gm
Dm7
Gm
Dm7
Play 3 times
Gm
Dm7
Gm
Dm7
Gm
Dm7
Gm
Dm
Gm

Dm7
Gm
F
E♭maj7
G
Gm
F
E♭maj7
Gm
C
Gm
B♭add13
E♭maj7
Gm
Dm
Gm
H
Fsus4
B♭
F/A
Gm7
Dm

Gm
Fsus4
B♭
F/A
Gm7
Dm
Gm
F
E♭maj7
I
Gm
F
E♭maj7
Gm
C
Gm
B♭7add13
E♭maj7
Gm
Dm7
Gm

J
Fsus4
B♭
F/A
Gm7
Dm
let ring
Gm
Fsus4
B♭
F/A
Gm7
Dm
Gm
F
E♭maj7
K
Gm
F
E♭maj7
Gm
C
Gm
B♭7add13
E♭maj7

Gm
Dm7
Gm
T
L
Dm7
Gm
Dm7
T
T
P
T
P
Gm
Dm7
Gm
T
P
Dm7
Gm
Dm7
T
T
T
T
Gm
Dm7
Gm
T
P
T
P

Dm7
Gm
T
P
Dm7
Gm
Dm7
Gm
Dm7
Gm
Dm7
Gm
T
T
T
P
T
T
P
Dm7
Gm

Dm7
Gm
Dm7
Gm
Dm7
Gm
Begin fade
Dm7
Gm
Dm7
Gm
Dm7
Fade out
Gm
Dm7
Gm

from Dave Grusin - *Mountain Dance*

Mountain Dance

By Dave Grusin

1.
C7
F
C
G♯°
Am
Dm
G
C5
2.
Dm
G
C
C
F
B♭
G
C
Play 3 times
F
B♭
C
To Coda

D
C/E F C/G Am C/E F G C Am C/E F Dm G C
C/E F C Am C/E F G C Am C/E F
1., 2., 3.
Dm G C
4., 6., 7., 9., 10., 11.
Dm G C
5., 8., 12., 13., 14., 15.
Dm G C
16.
Dm G C C/E F C Am C/E F G C
Am C/E F Dm G C C7 F C G♯° Am

E
Dm G C F B♭ C
C5
3
F
C5
D.S. al Coda
C
Bass: w/ Bass Fig. 1 (6 times)
6
C7 F C G♯° Am Dm G C

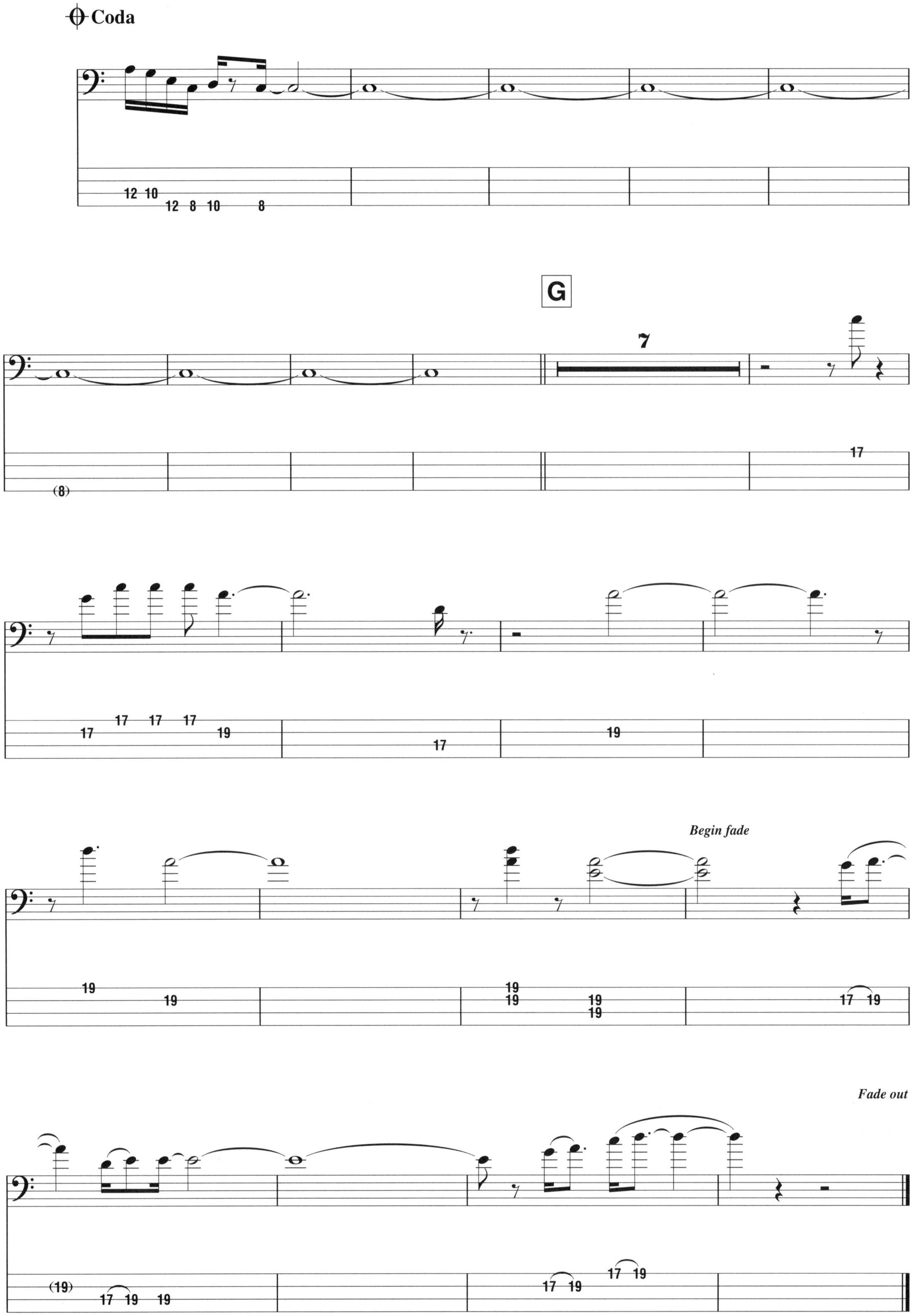
Coda
G
7
Begin fade
Fade out

from M^2

Nikki's Groove

By Marcus Miller

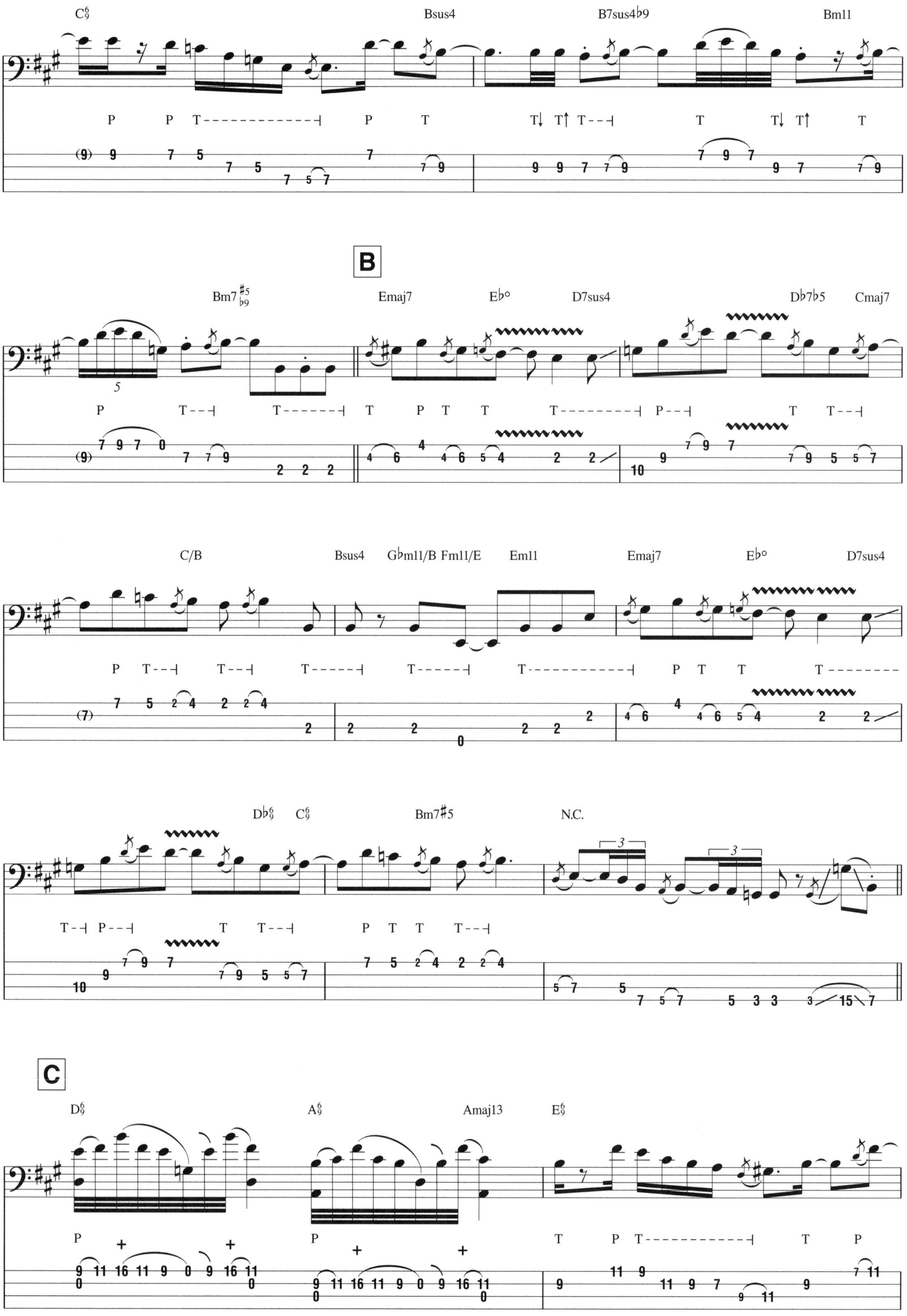
C6/9
Bsus4
B7sus4♭9
Bm11
B
Bm7♯5♭9
Emaj7
E♭°
D7sus4
D♭7♭5
Cmaj7
C/B
Bsus4
G♭m11/B
Fm11/E
Em11
Emaj7
E♭°
D7sus4
D♭6/9
C6/9
Bm7♯5
N.C.
C
D6/9
A6/9
Amaj13
E6/9

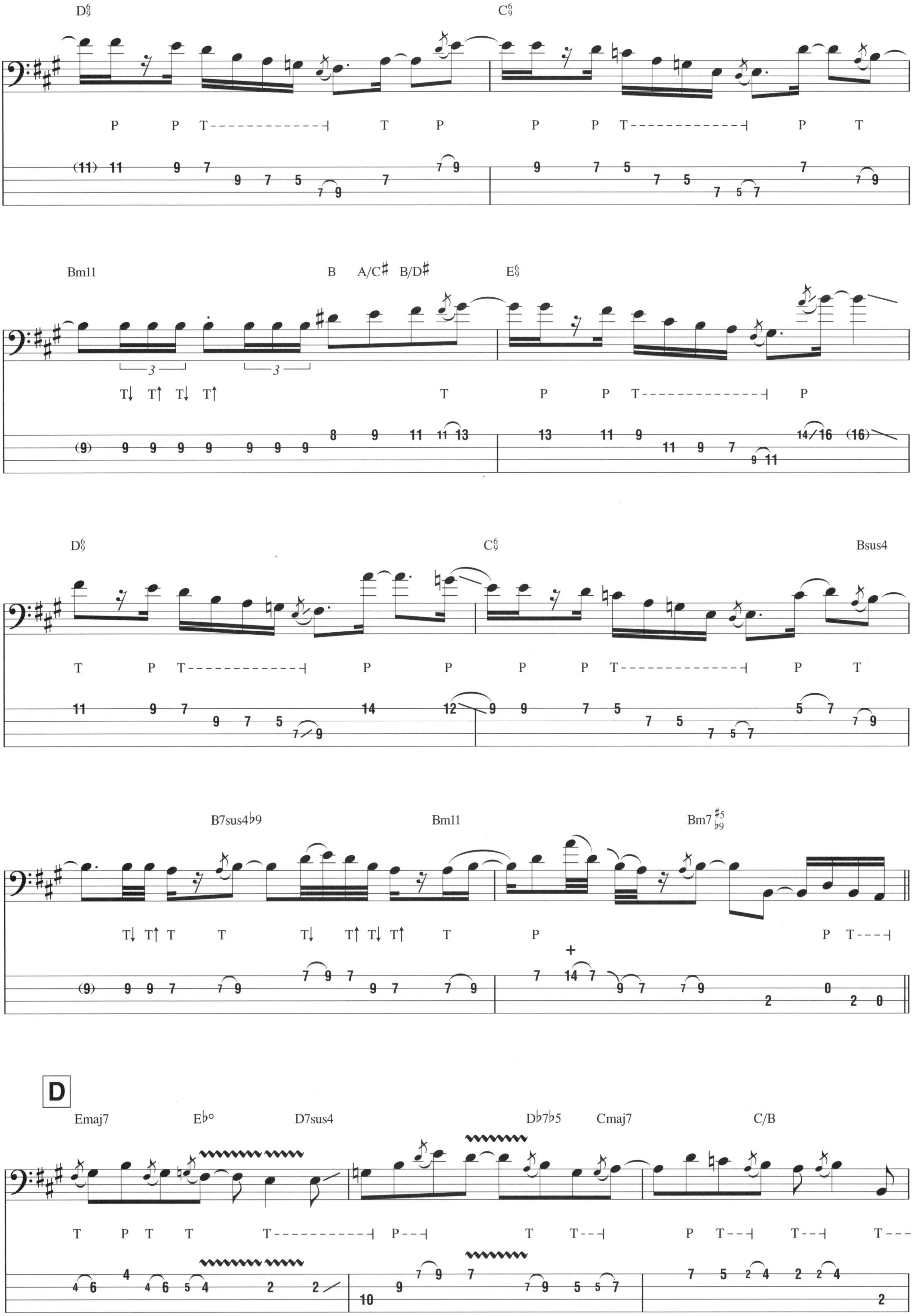
D6/9
C6/9
Bm11
B
A/C♯
B/D♯
E6/9
D6/9
C6/9
Bsus4
B7sus4♭9
Bm11
Bm7♯5♭9
D
Emaj7
E♭°
D7sus4
D♭7♭5
Cmaj7
C/B

Bsus4
G♭m11/B Fm11/E
Em11
Emaj7
E♭°
D7sus4
D♭⁶₉ C⁶₉
Bm7♯5
N.C.
E
Em11
D
Cmaj7
Bmaj7
B7
Em11
D
Cmaj7

To Coda
Bm7
C/B
Bm11
B7♭9♯5
F
E6/9
D6/9
C6/9
B7sus4
8va
loco
B7
B
A/C♯
B/D♯
E6/9
D6/9
8va
C6/9
loco

Bm11
G
Emaj7
E♭°
D7sus4
D♭7♭5
Cmaj7
Bsus4♭9
Bsus4
G♭m11/B Fm11/E
Em11
Emaj7
E♭°
D7sus4
D♭6/9
C6/9
Bm7♯5
N.C.
D.S. al Coda

Coda

*This is a combination of harp harm. and natural harm. At 5th fret place fingers as if striking a natural harmonic and pluck the strings using harp harm. technique.

from *The Sun Don't Lie*

Panther

By Marcus Miller

B
Em
P
C
Em7
Em7♭6
8va
steady gliss.
3
Em11
Am
Am7
Bm7
Em9♭6
G7
H.H.
*Hypothetical fret location.
Cmaj9
1/4

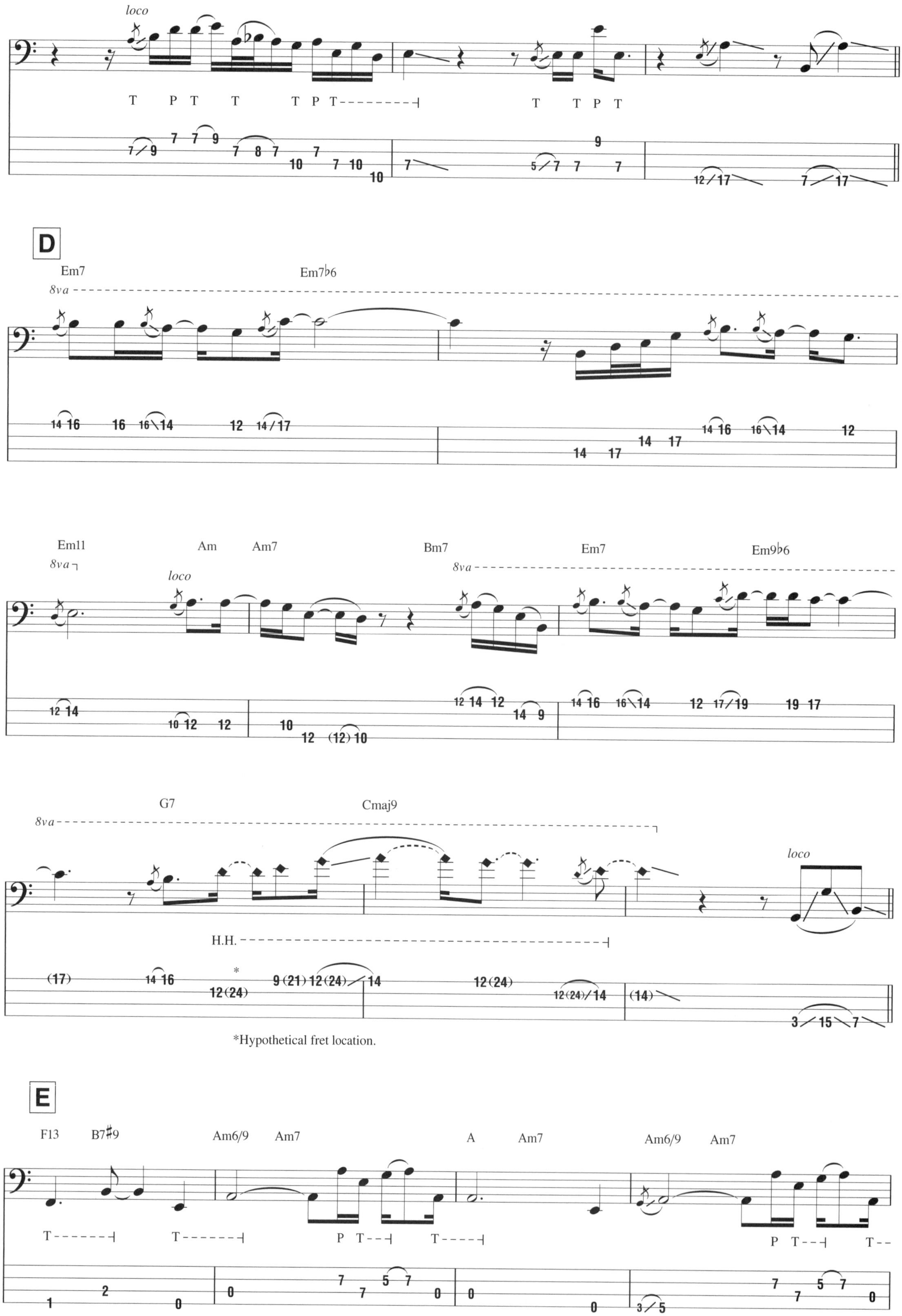

*Hypothetical fret location.

F
A
Am7
Em
let ring
G
Em7
Em7♭6
Em11
Am
P.M.
Am7
Bm7
G7/A♭

Cmaj9
Em
P.M.
H
Em7
Em7♭6
Em11
Am
Am7
Bm7
Em7
Em7♭6
G7
I
Cmaj9
F13
B7♯9
Am6/9
Am7

*Hypothetical fret location.

K
Em
8va
loco

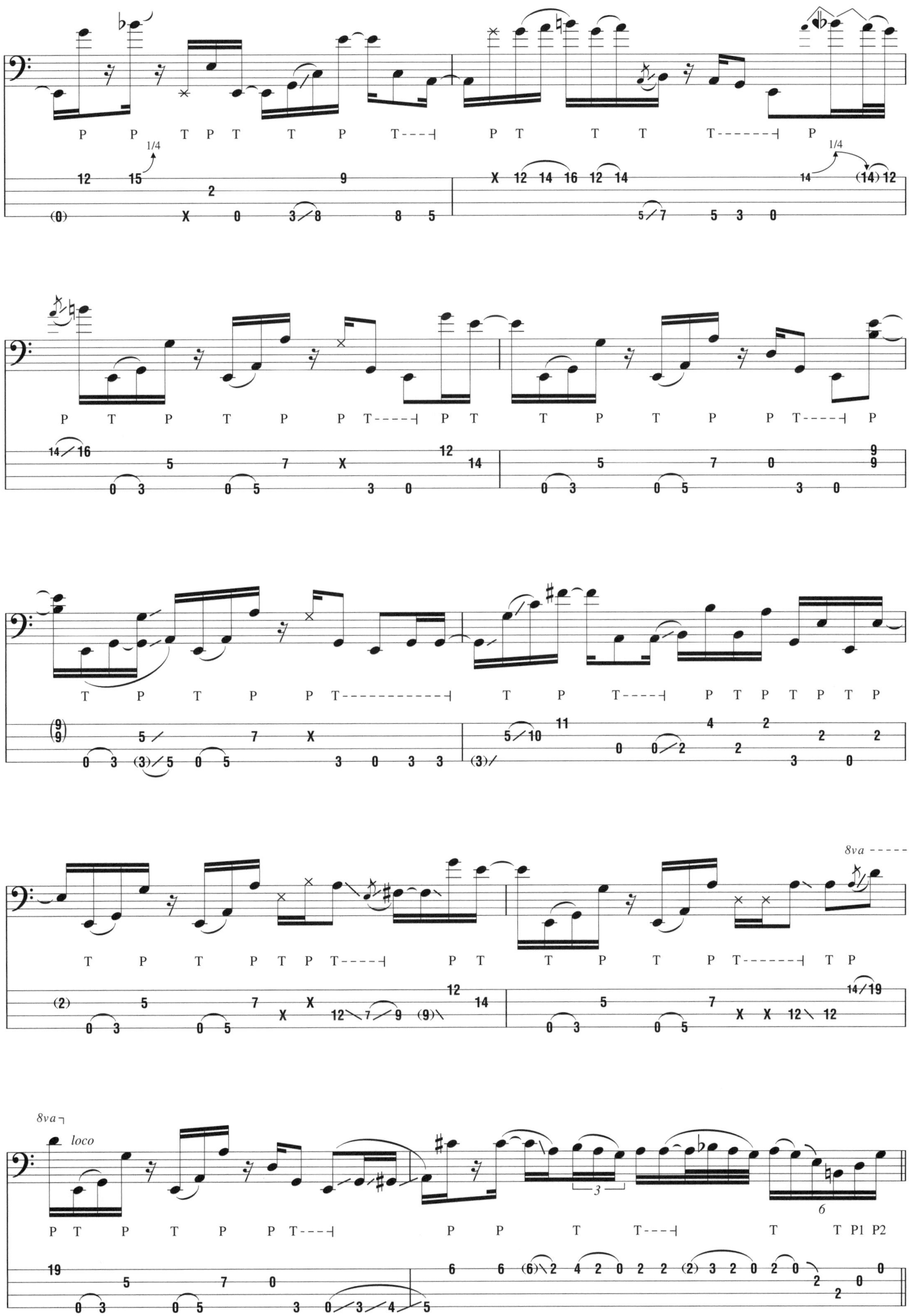
8va
loco

L
Em
T
Harm.
P T
P T Harm.
P1 P2 P1 P2 P1 P2
8va
loco
Harm.
Pitch: G D A
G D A
D A
Pitch: A D
M
E
T
P P T

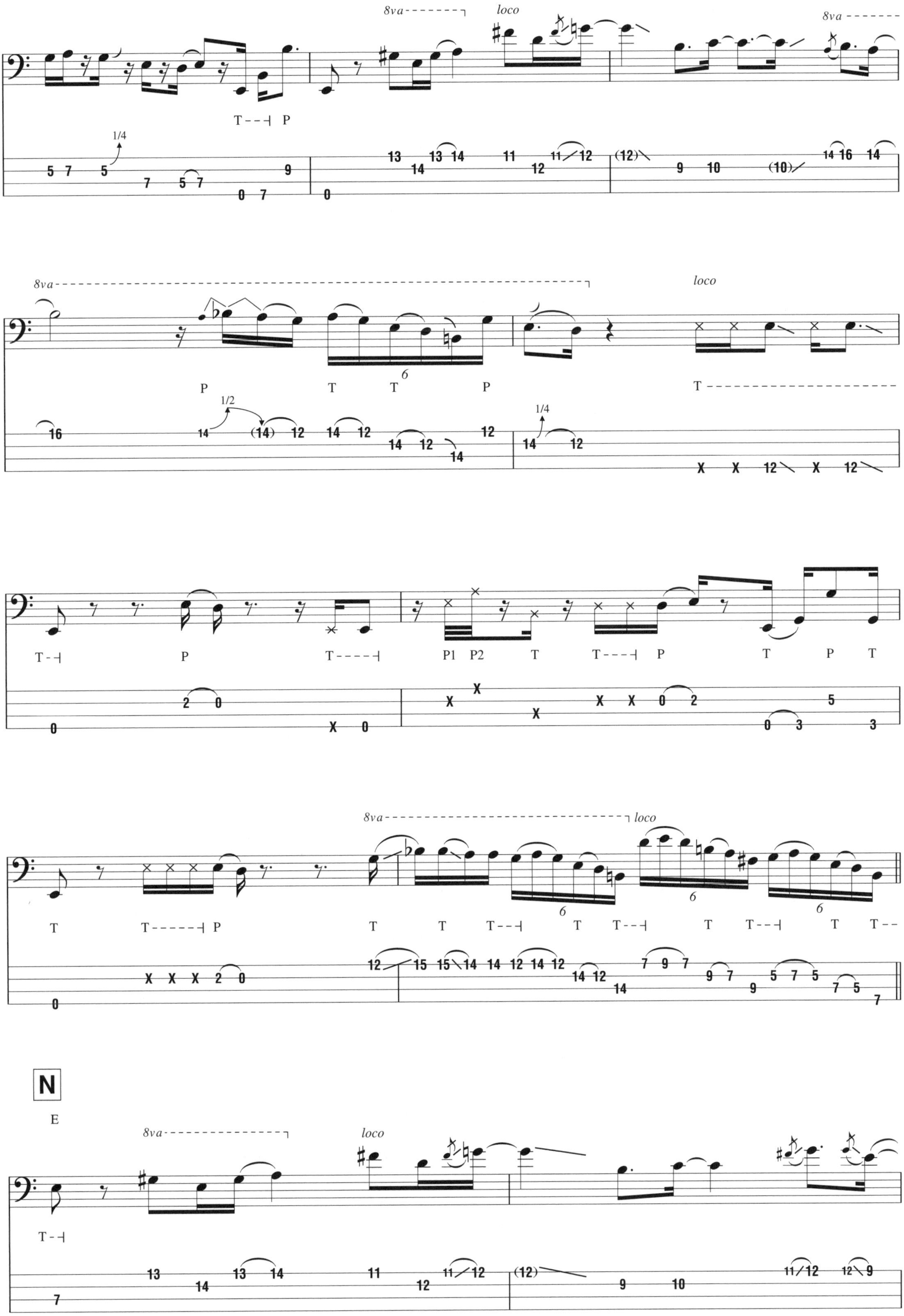
8va
loco
1/4
1/2
N
E

8va
loco
Begin fade
8va
loco
Fade out

from M^2

Power

Words and Music by Marcus Miller

A

Moderate Funk ♩ = 88

B
Bm
A
Bass 1
Synth. bass
mf
Bm
A
Bm
Amaj9
Bm

Bm
A
Bass 1
Bass 2
Bass Fig. 1
End Bass Fig. 1
mf
Synth. bass
Bass 2: w/ Bass Fig. 1
Bm
A
Bass 1
Synth. bass
Bm
Amaj9
Bm

C
Synth. bass tacet
A
G
A
Asus2
Bass 1
let ring
F#7
F#7b5
Bm
A
G
A
Asus2
F#7
F#7b5
Bm
A
Bass 1
Synth. bass
D
Bm
A

Bass 2: w/ Bass Fig. 1
Bm
A
Bm
Amaj9
Bm
E
Bm9
A6/9
Gmaj7♯11
mp
mp

F
E5
F♯m7
Bm
Synth. bass tacet
Bass 1
Bass 1
Synth. bass
Bass 1

Bass 1
Synth. bass

G
Bm
A
Bm
A
Bm
Amaj9

Bm
H
A
let ring
G
let ring
A
Asus2
F#7
Bm
A
let ring
G
let ring
A
Asus2

F♯7
Bm
A
I
Bm

J
Bass 2: w/ Bass Fig. 1 (2 times)
Bm
A
Bm
A
Bm
A

Bm
K
Bm
Bass 1 tacet
Synth. bass
N.C.
(Synth. and drums)

from *The Sun Don't Lie*

Rampage

By Marcus Miller

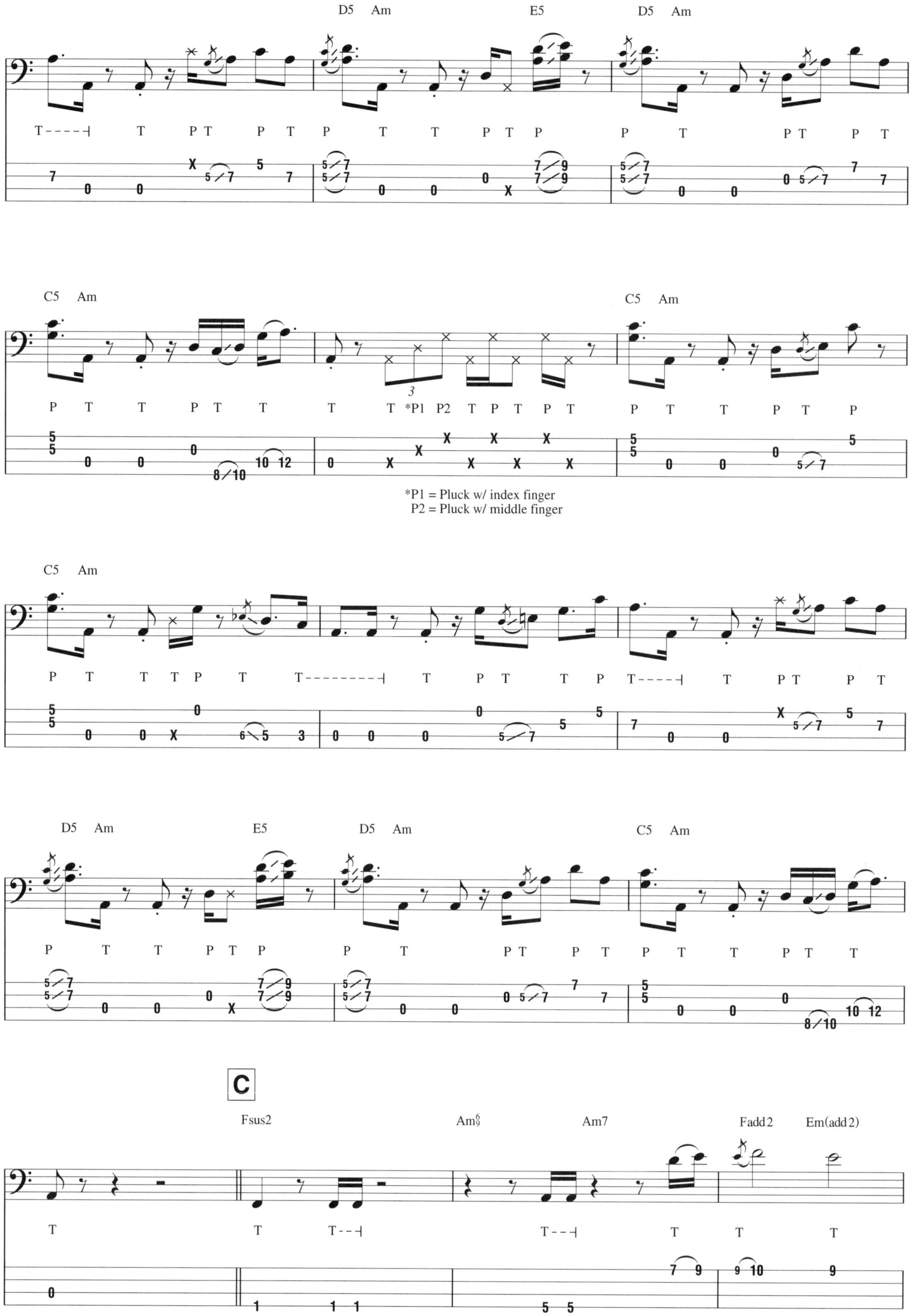
D5 Am E5 D5 Am
C5 Am C5 Am
*P1 = Pluck w/ index finger
P2 = Pluck w/ middle finger
C5 Am
D5 Am E5 D5 Am C5 Am
C
Fsus2 Am6/9 Am7 Fadd2 Em(add2)

B♭/D
C6
G/B
E7♯9/G♯
F
D
E7♯9
C5
Am
C5
Am
D5
Am
E5
D5
Am
C5
Am
E
C5
Am
C5
Am

D5 Am
E5
D5 Am
C5 Am
C5 Am
C5 Am
D5 Am
E5
D5 Am
C5 Am
F
Fsus2
Am6/9
Am7
Fadd2
Em(add2)

B♭/D
C6
G/B
E7♯9/G♯
F6/9
G
E7♯9
C5
Am
let ring
D5
E5
T*⊕

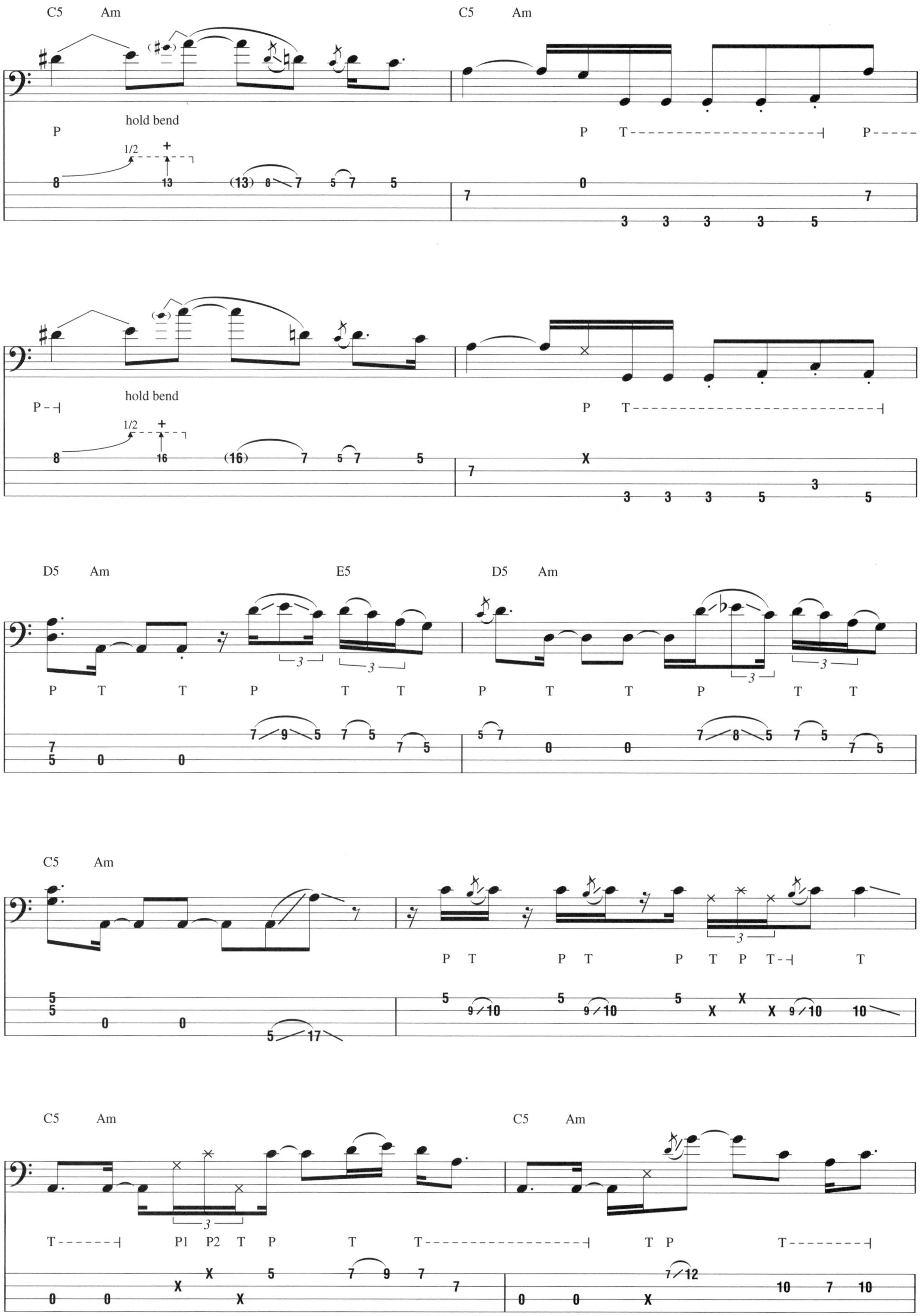
C5 Am
C5 Am
hold bend
1/2
hold bend
1/2
D5 Am
E5
D5 Am
C5 Am
C5 Am
C5 Am

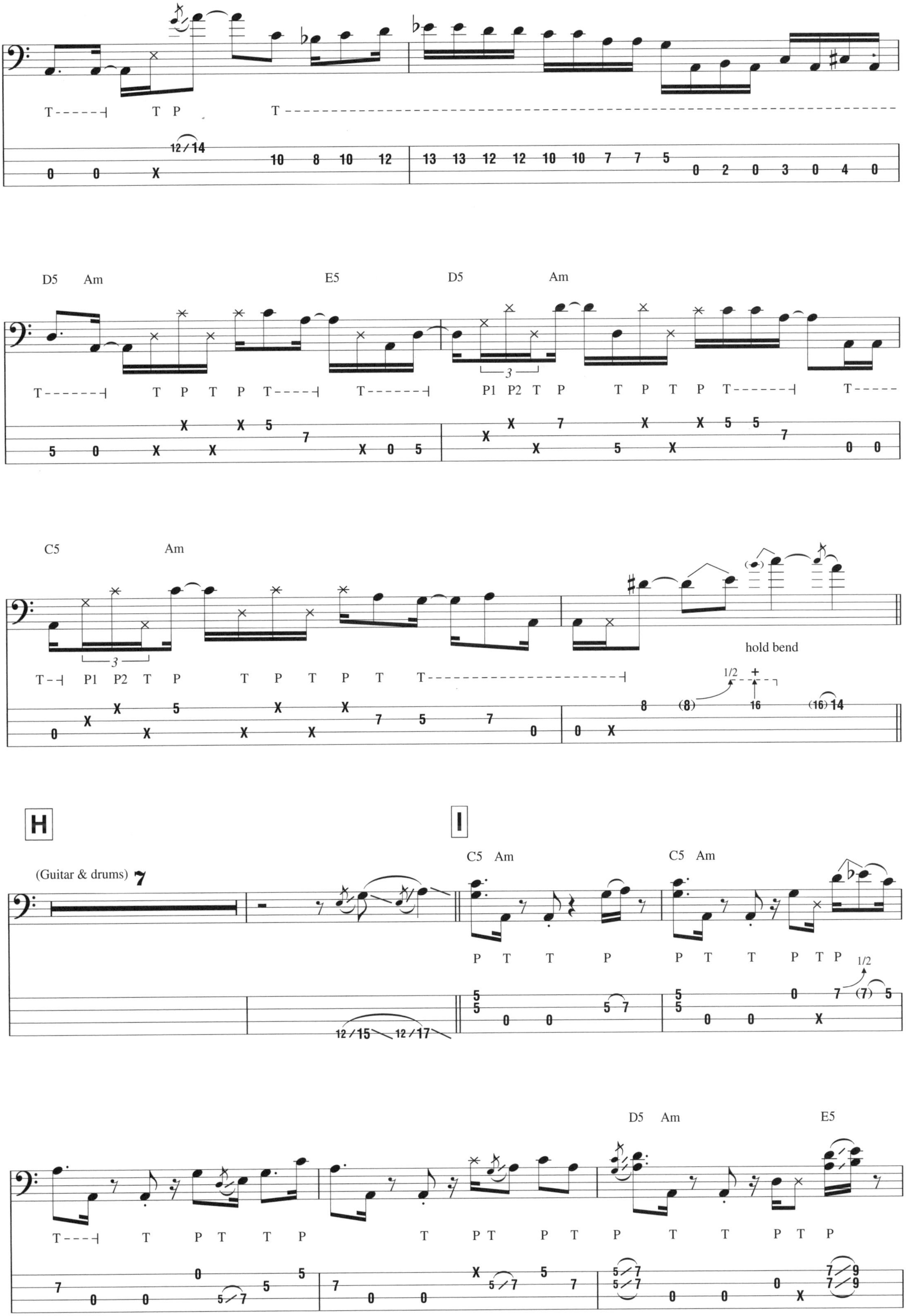
D5 Am E5 D5 Am
C5 Am
hold bend
H
(Guitar & drums)
I
C5 Am C5 Am
D5 Am E5

D5 Am
C5 Am
J
Fsus2
Am6/9
Am7
Fadd2
Em(add2)
B♭/D
C6
G/B
E7♯9/G♯
F6/9
E7♯9
mp
K
C5 Am
C5 Am
mf
D5 Am
E5
D5 Am

C5 Am
C5 Am
C5 Am
D5 Am
E5
D5 Am
C5 Am
C5 Am
C5 Am
D5 Am
E5

D5 Am
C5 Am
C5 Am
C5 Am
D5 Am
E5
D5 Am
C5 Am
C5 Am
C5 Am
Begin fade
D5 Am
E5
D5 Am
C5 Am
mp
Fade out
C5 Am
C5 Am

from Lee Ritenour - *Rio*

Rio Funk

By Lee Ritenour

C
B♭
F5
T
P
P
P
P
T
P
T
T
(3)
Gm7
F
Gm
T
P
P
P
P
B
Gm
C7
Gm
T
P
T
P
P
T
P
T
C7
Gm
C7
T
P
T
T
P
T
P
P
T
Gm
C7
Gm
T
P
T
P
P
P
T
T
P
T

C7
Gm
C7
Gm
C7
Gm
C
C6
C♯6
D6
Bm
Em9
Bm
Em9
A7sus4

F#7#9
Bm7
E9
let ring
let ring
let ring
let ring
Bm
Em9
Bm
Em9
A7sus4
F#7#9
Bm7
let ring
let ring
let ring
let ring
C6/9/D
G7sus4
C9
C#9
D9

D
Gm7
C
B♭
F
Gm7
F♯
Gm7
C
B♭
F
Gm7
F
Gm
E
Gm
C7
Gm

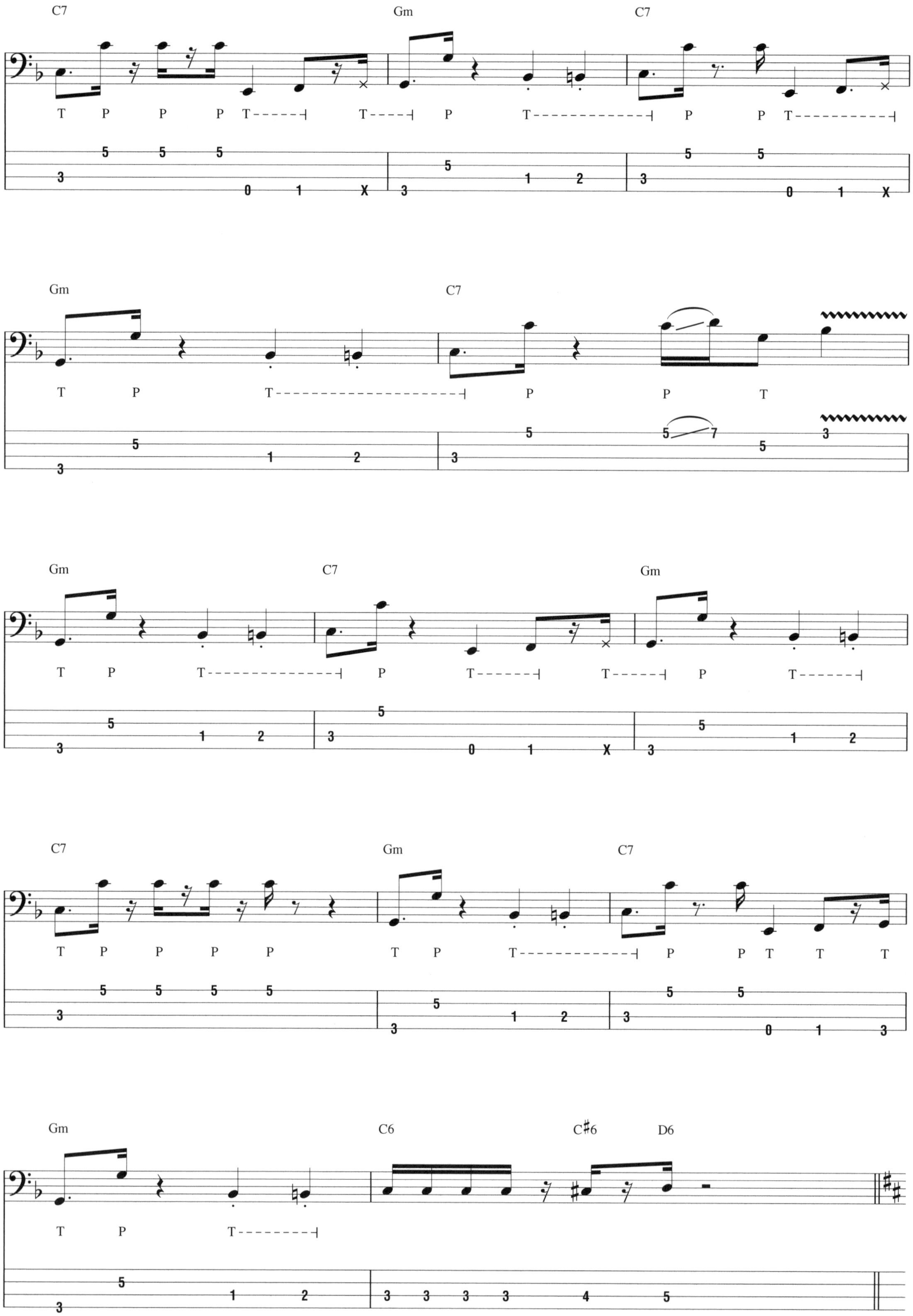
C7
Gm
C7
T P P P T T P T P P T
Gm
C7
T P T P P T
Gm
C7
Gm
T P T P T T P T
C7
Gm
C7
T P P P P T P T P P T T T
Gm
C6
C#6
D6
T P T

F

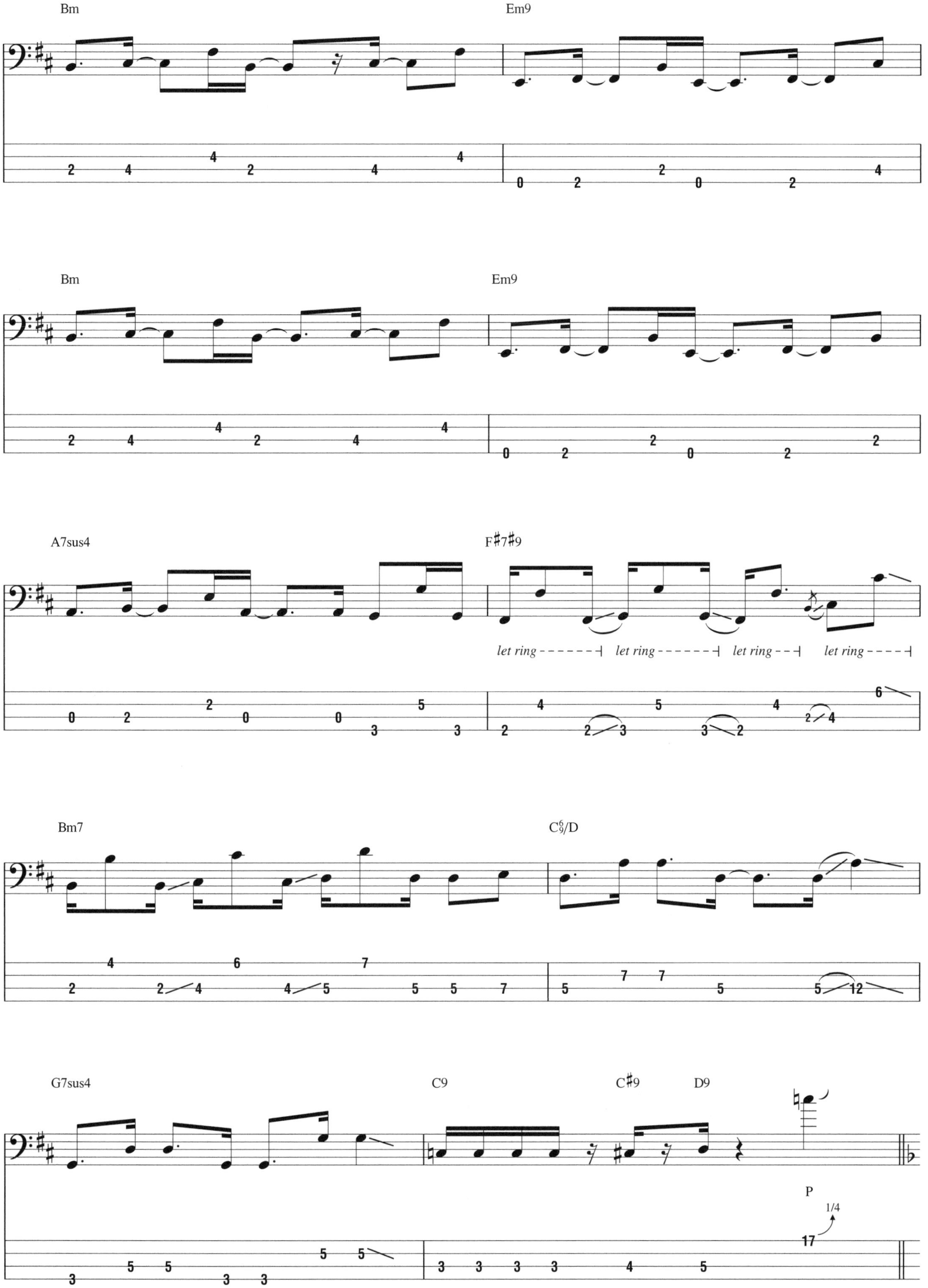
Bm
Em9
Bm
Em9
A7sus4
F♯7♯9
let ring
let ring
let ring
let ring
Bm7
C6/9/D
G7sus4
C9
C♯9
D9
P
1/4

*P1 = Pluck w/ index finger
P2 = Pluck w/ 2nd finger

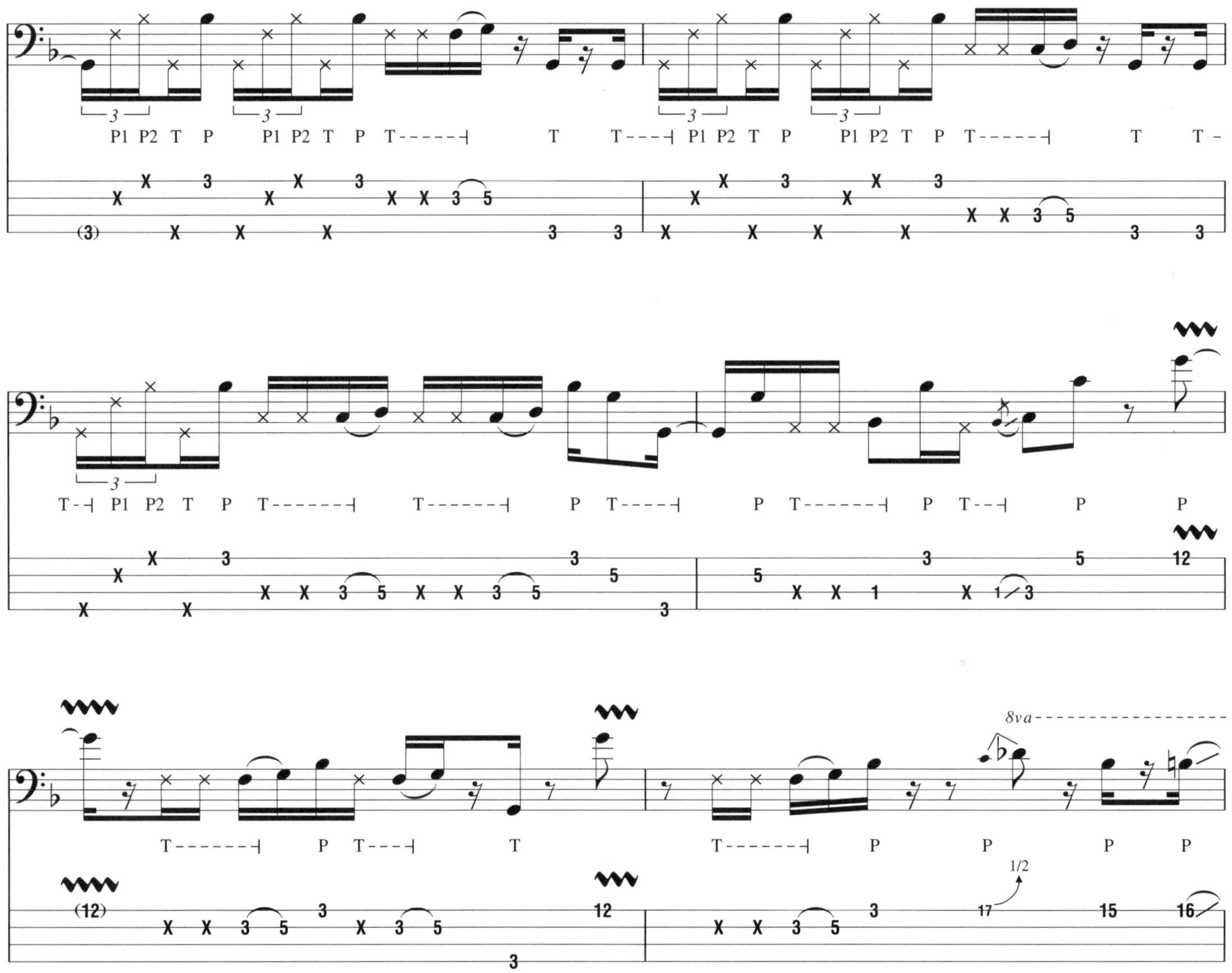

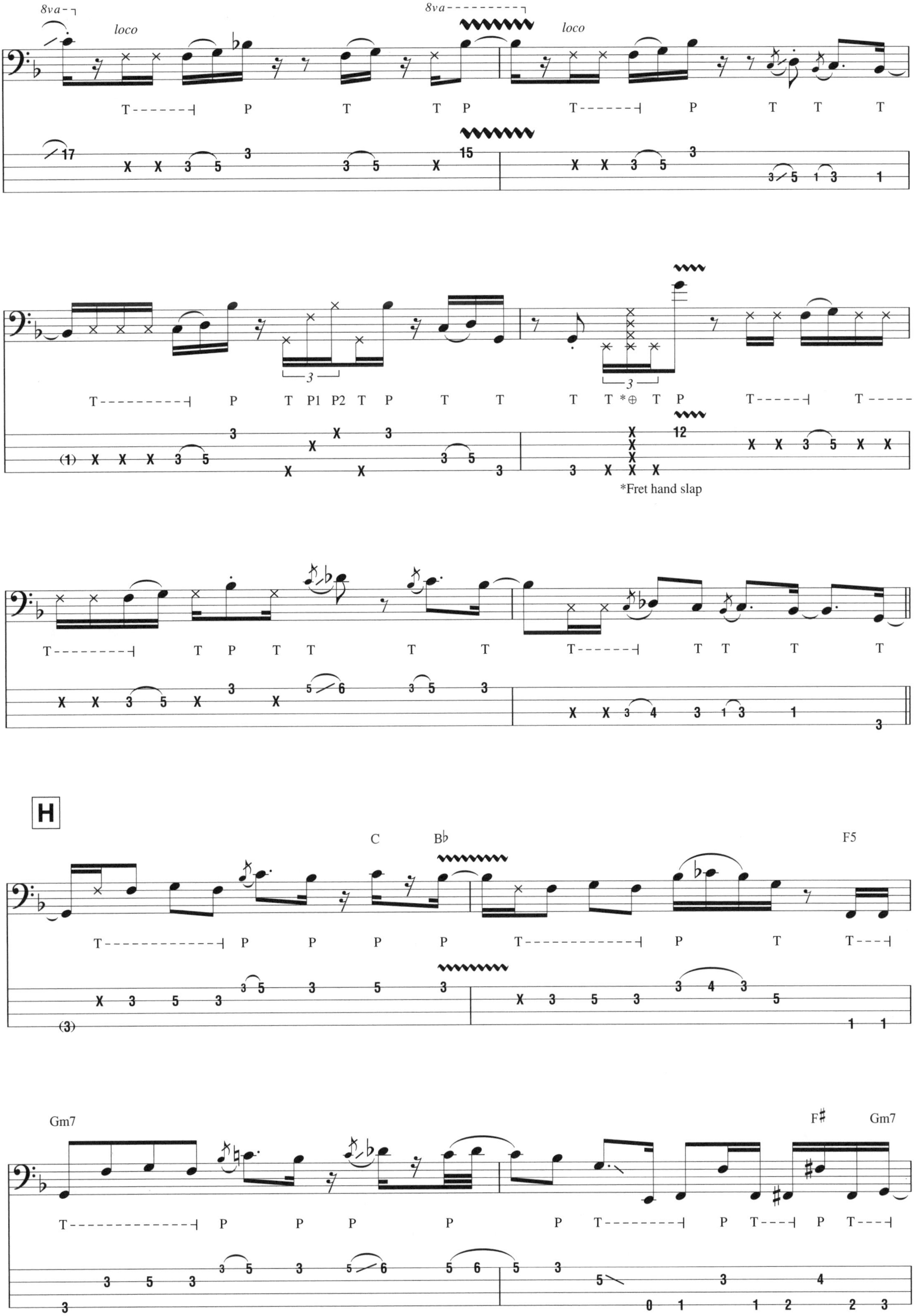
8va
loco
8va
loco
*Fret hand slap
H
C
B♭
F5
Gm7
F♯
Gm7

C
B♭
F♯
Gm7
F
Gm
I
Gm
C7
Gm
C7
Gm
C7
Gm
C7
Gm

C7
Gm
C7
T P P T P T P T T T
Gm
C7
Gm
T P T P P T P T
J
C6
C#6
D6
Bm
Em9
T T T
Bm
Em9
A7sus4
F#7#9
let ring
let ring
let ring
let ring

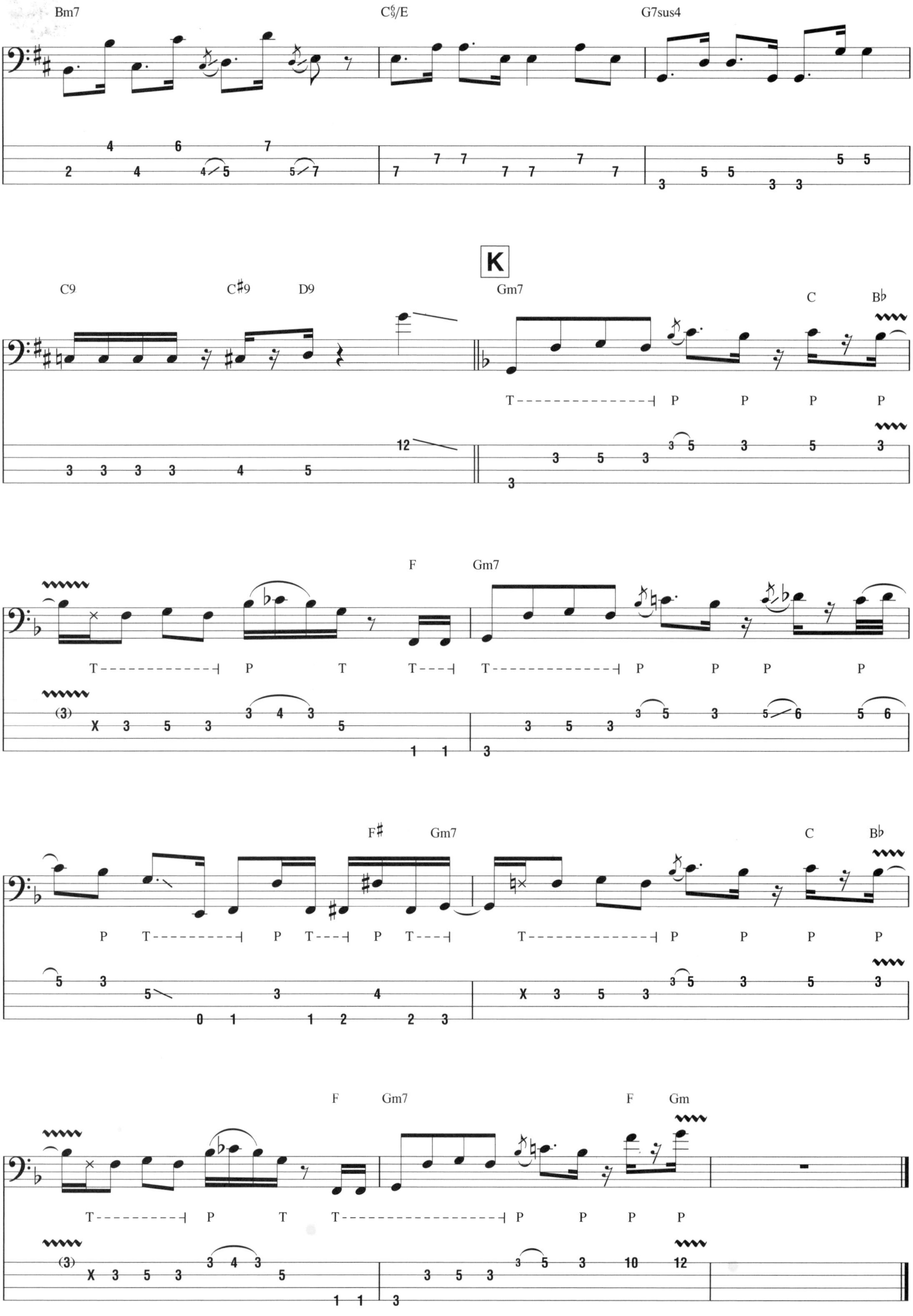
Bm7
C6/9/E
G7sus4
K
C9
C#9
D9
Gm7
C
B♭
F
Gm7
F#
Gm7
C
B♭
F
Gm7
F
Gm

from David Sanborn - *Straight to the Heart*

Run for Cover

Words and Music by Marcus Miller

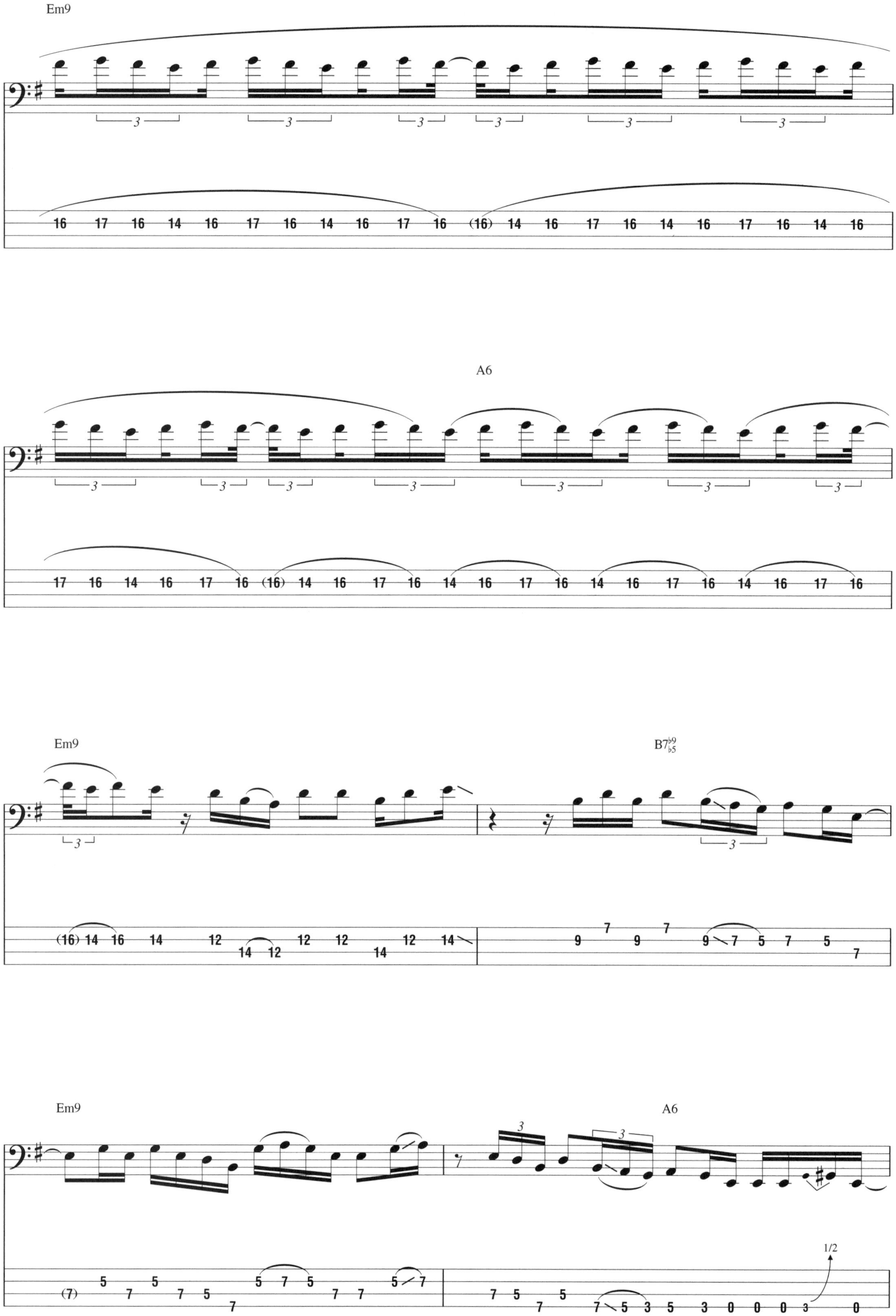
Em9
A6
Em9
B7♭9♭5
Em9
A6
1/2

Em9
B7♭9♭5
Em9
A6
Em9
B7♭9♭5
Em9
A6
Em9
B7♭9♭5
P
T
1/2

C
Em9
N.C.
N.C.

D
Em11
C/D
N.C.
Em9
*Fret hand slap.
Em11
C/D
N.C.
Em9
B7

E
C
Am7
Em7
C
Am7
B7sus4
B7♭9♭5
F
Em11
C/D
N.C.
Em9

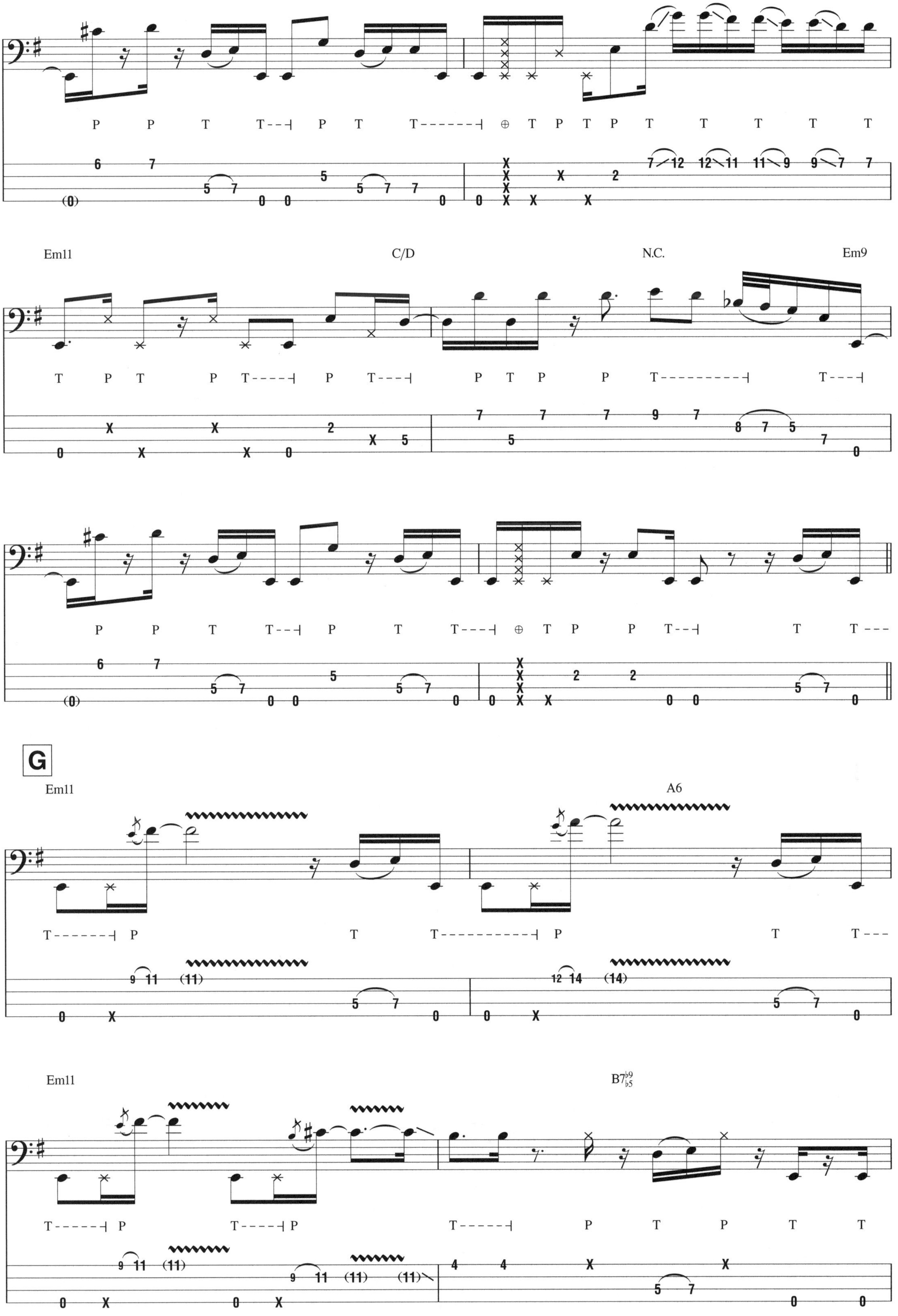
Em11
C/D
N.C.
Em9
G
Em11
A6
Em11
B7♭9♭5

Em11
A6
Em11
B7♭9♭5
Em11
A6
Em11
B7♭9♭5
1/2
1/2

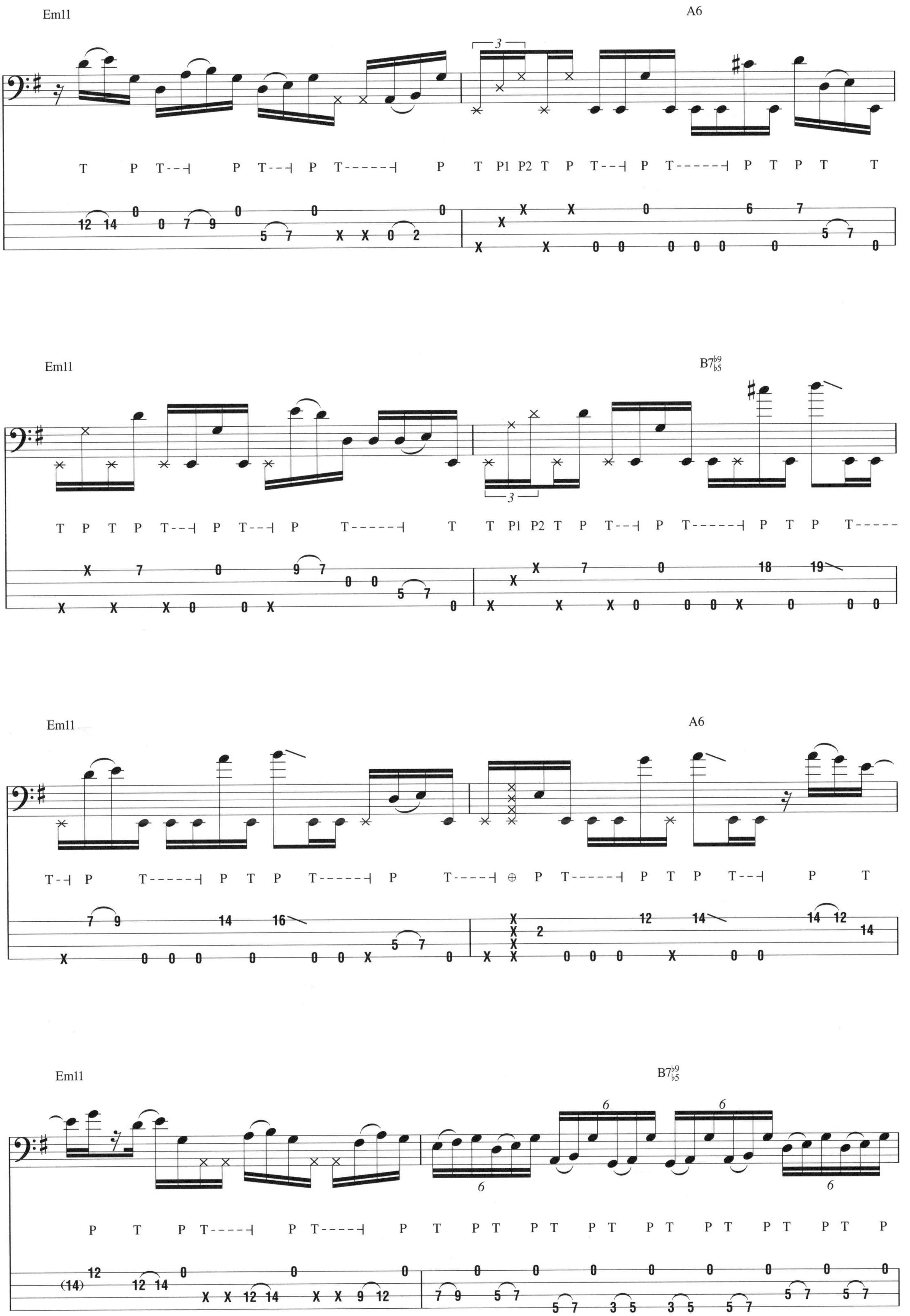
Em11
A6
Em11
B7♭9♭5
Em11
A6
Em11
B7♭9♭5

Em11
A6
Em11
B7♭9♭5
*Thumb sixteenth notes while sliding down the neck.
H
Em9
A6
Em9
B7♭9♭5
Em9
A6

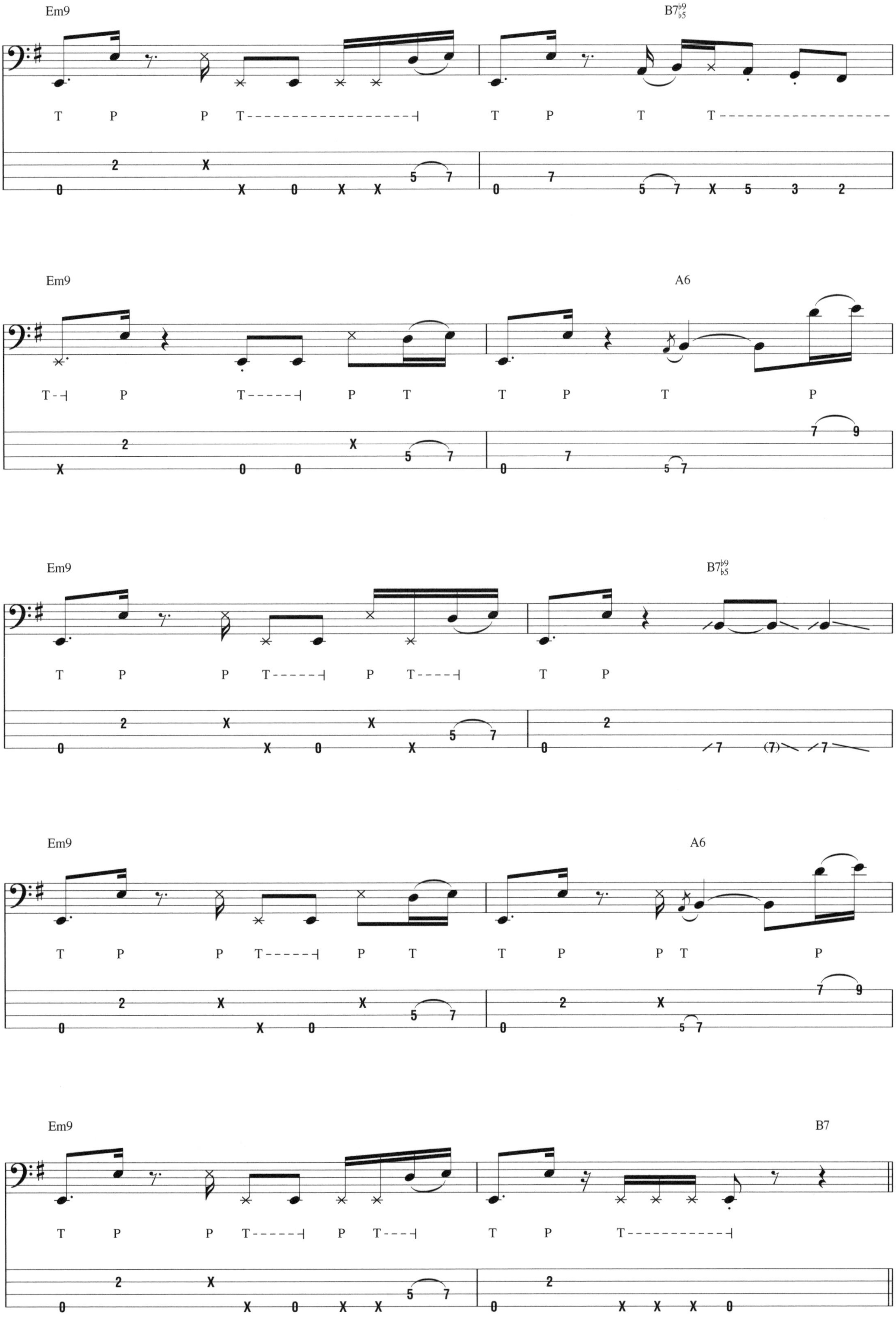
Em9
B7♭9♭5
Em9
A6
Em9
B7♭9♭5
Em9
A6
Em9
B7

I
C
Am7
Em7
C
Am7
B7sus4
B7♭9♭5
1/2
J
Em11
C/D
N.C.
Em9

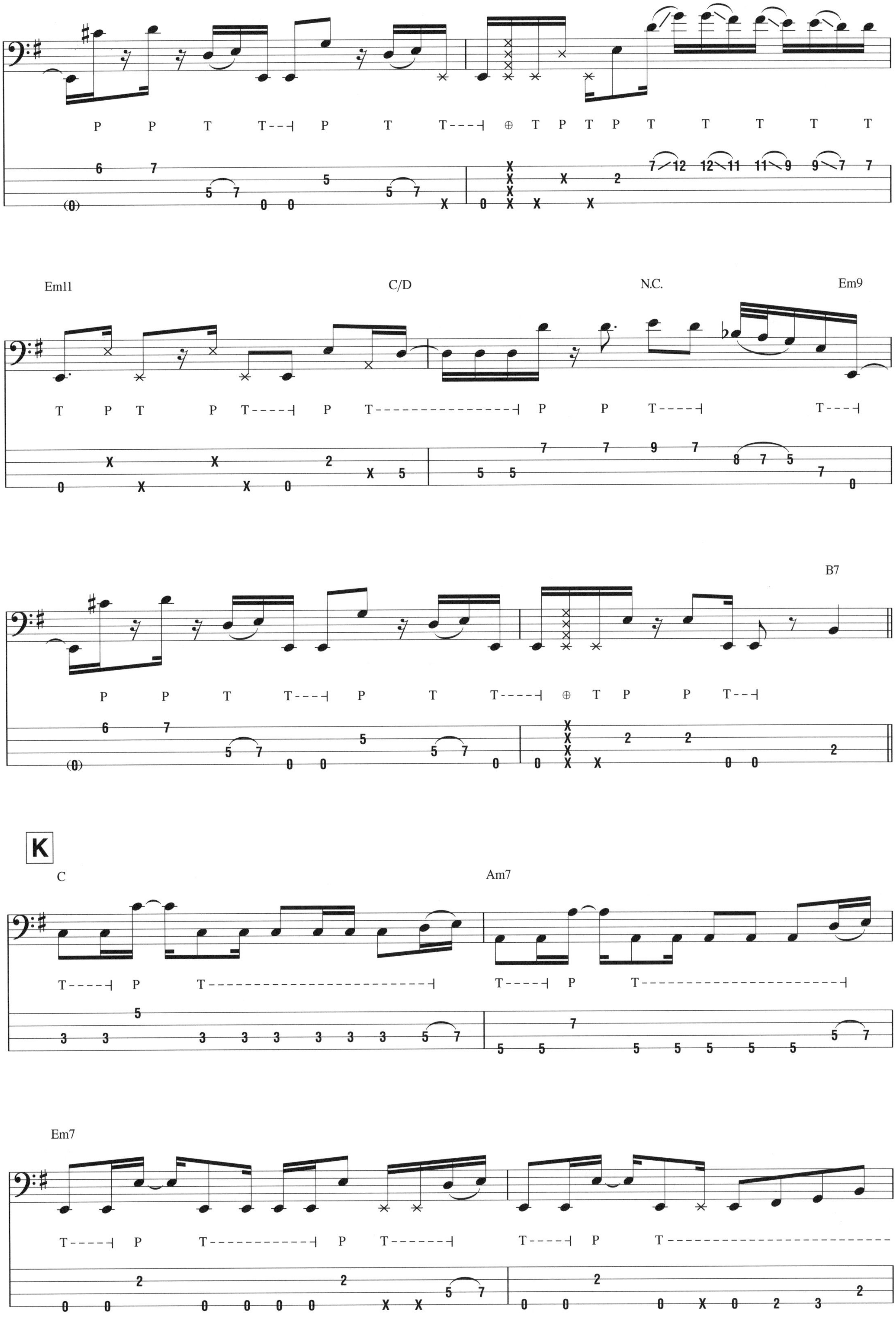
Em11
C/D
N.C.
Em9
B7
K
C
Am7
Em7

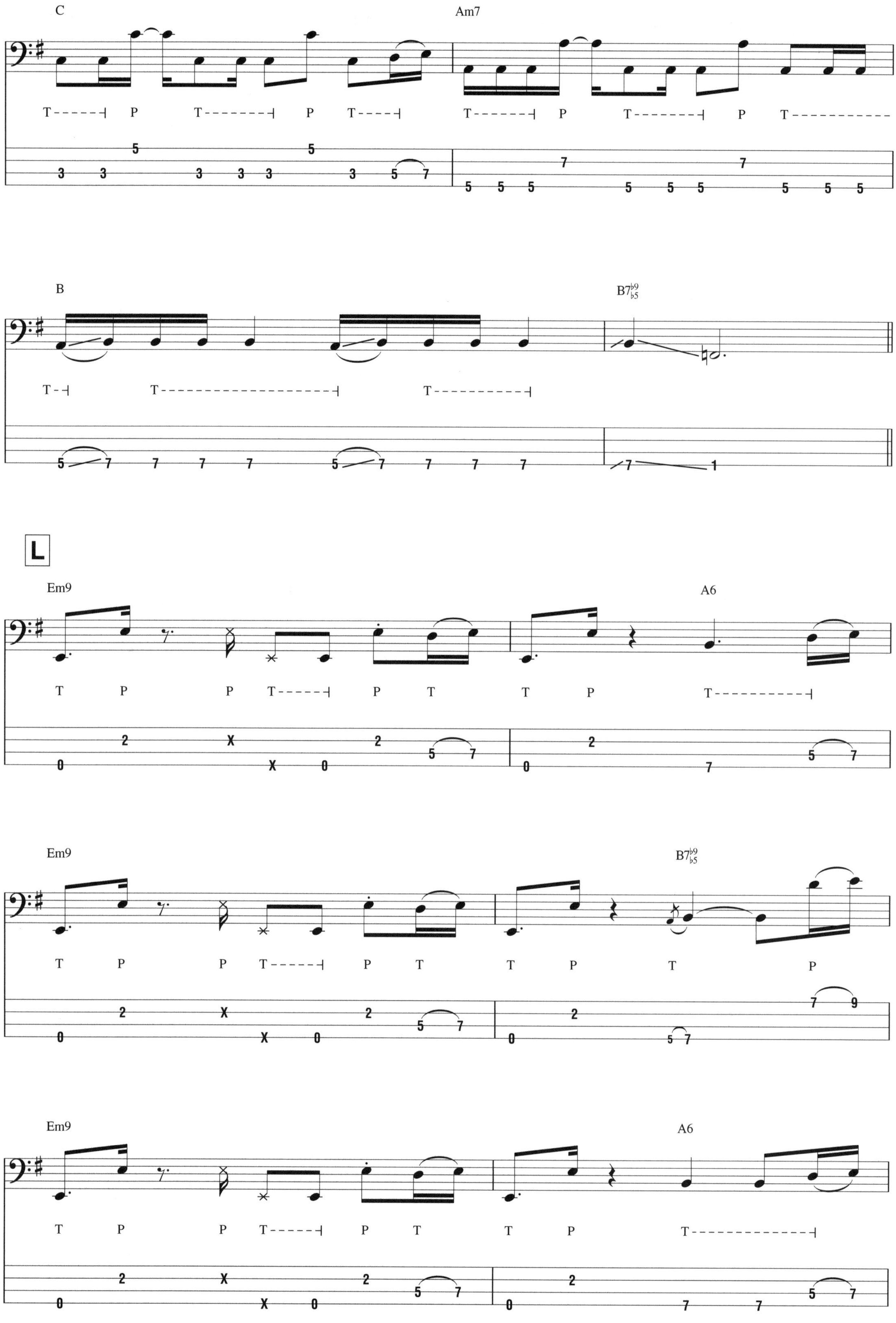
C
Am7
B
B7b9b5
L
Em9
A6
Em9
B7b9b5
Em9
A6

Em9
B7♭9♭5
Em9
A6
Em9
B7♭9♭5
Em9
A6
Em9
B7♭9♭5
Em9
A6

Em9
B7♭9♭5
Em9
A6
Em9
B7♭9♭5
Em11
C/D
B7♭9♭5
Free time
Em11
p
mf

from *The Sun Don't Lie*

Scoop

By Marcus Miller

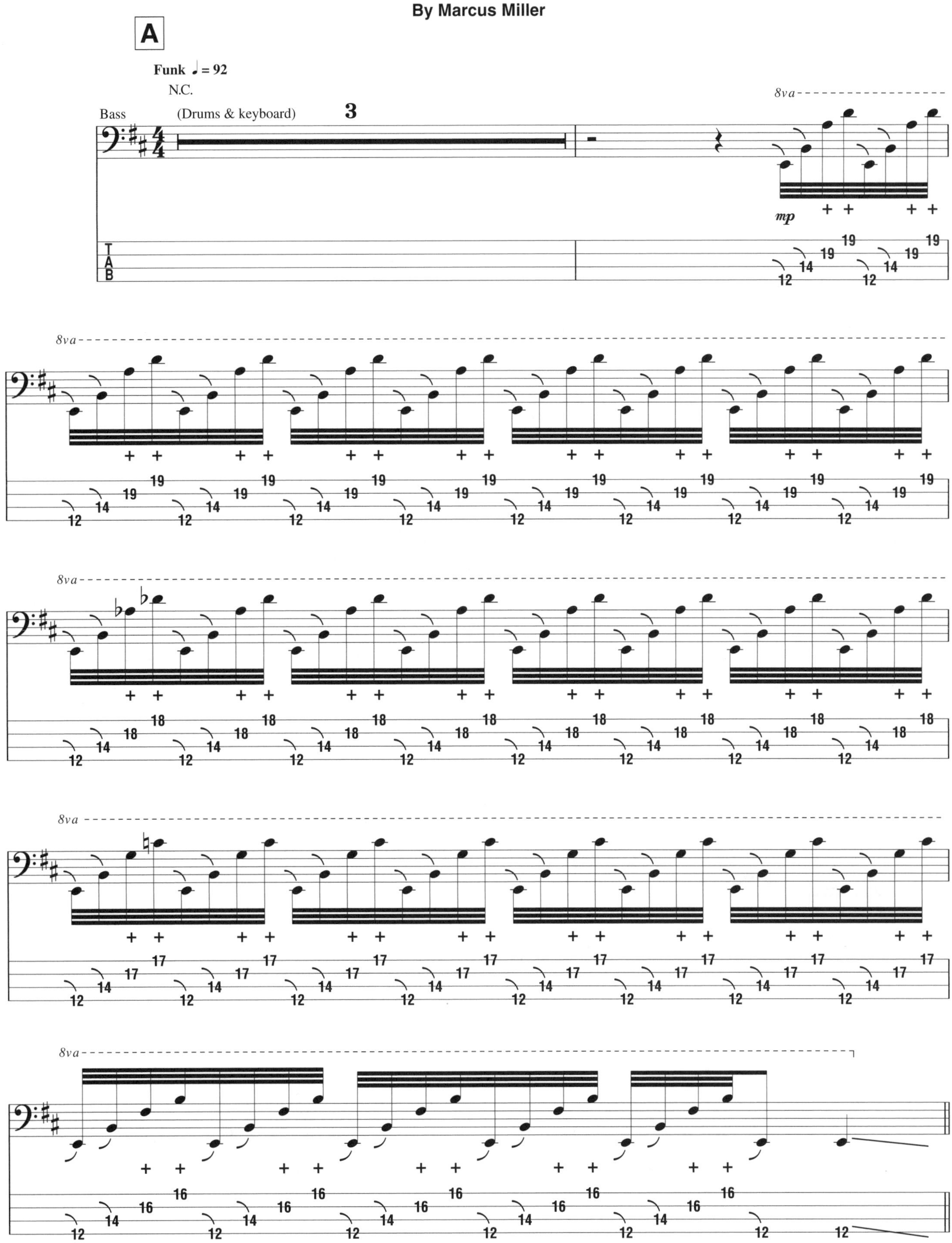

*Plucked w/ thumb & index finger.

Bm7add4
B♭m7add4
Am7add4
let ring
E
Bm7add4
B♭m7add4
E5
D5
A5
G5
E7sus4
E13
D6
Dsus2
E7sus4
E13
N.C. (D6)

D
E
*Plucked w/ thumb & index finger.
Bm7add4
B♭m7add4
Am7add4
Am6
Am
E
Bm7add4
B♭m7add4
Am6
Am
E
E7sus4
E6/9
E7sus4
E6/9
E7sus4
E6/9

Am7add6
E7sus4
E6/9
E7sus4
E6/9
E7sus4
E6/9
Am7add6
F
C7♯9
E♭
F
C7♯9
A5
B♭5
B

G
E7sus4
E6/9
E7sus4
E6/9
E7sus4
E6/9
Am7add6
H
N.C.
*Fret hand slap.

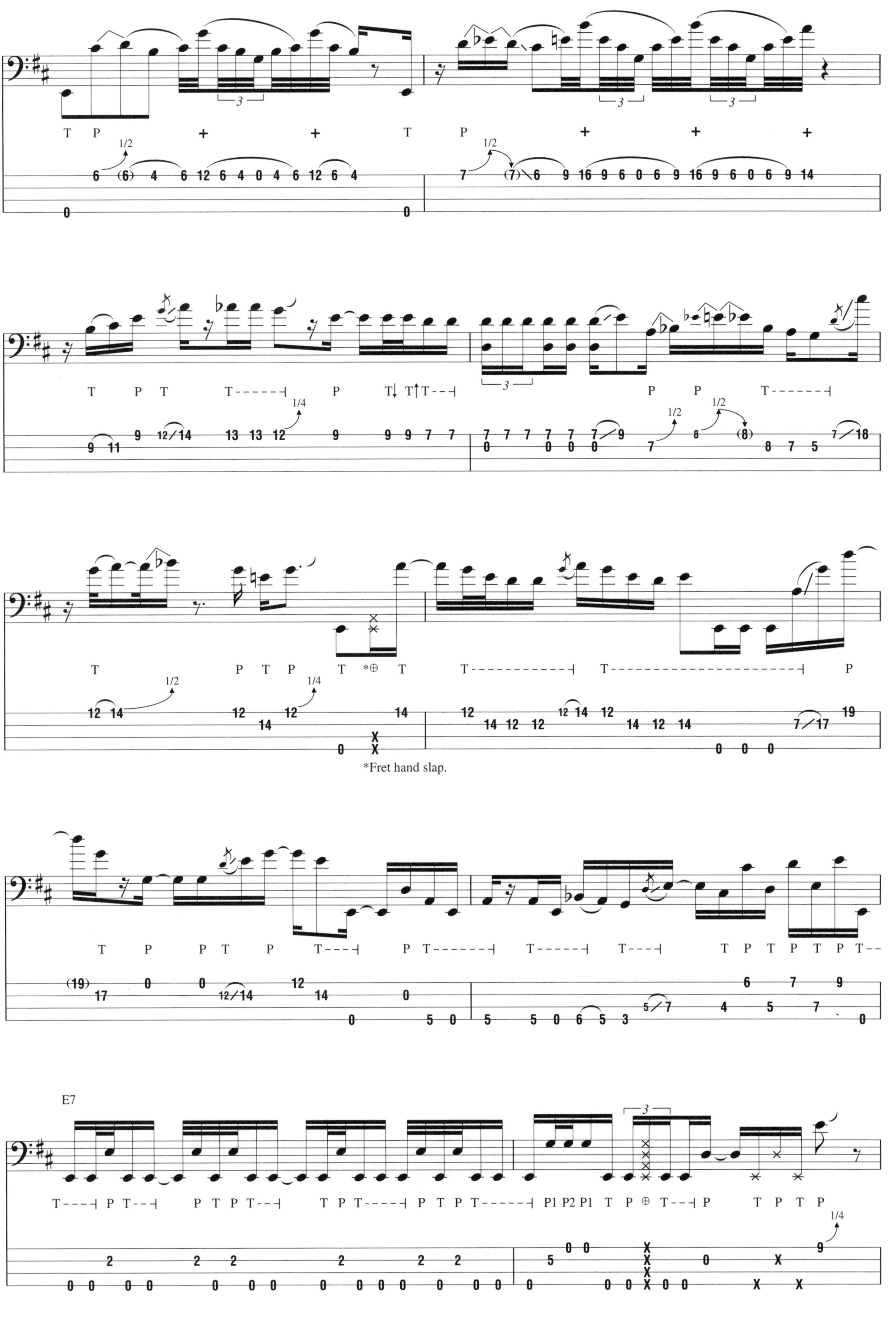
*Fret hand slap.
E7

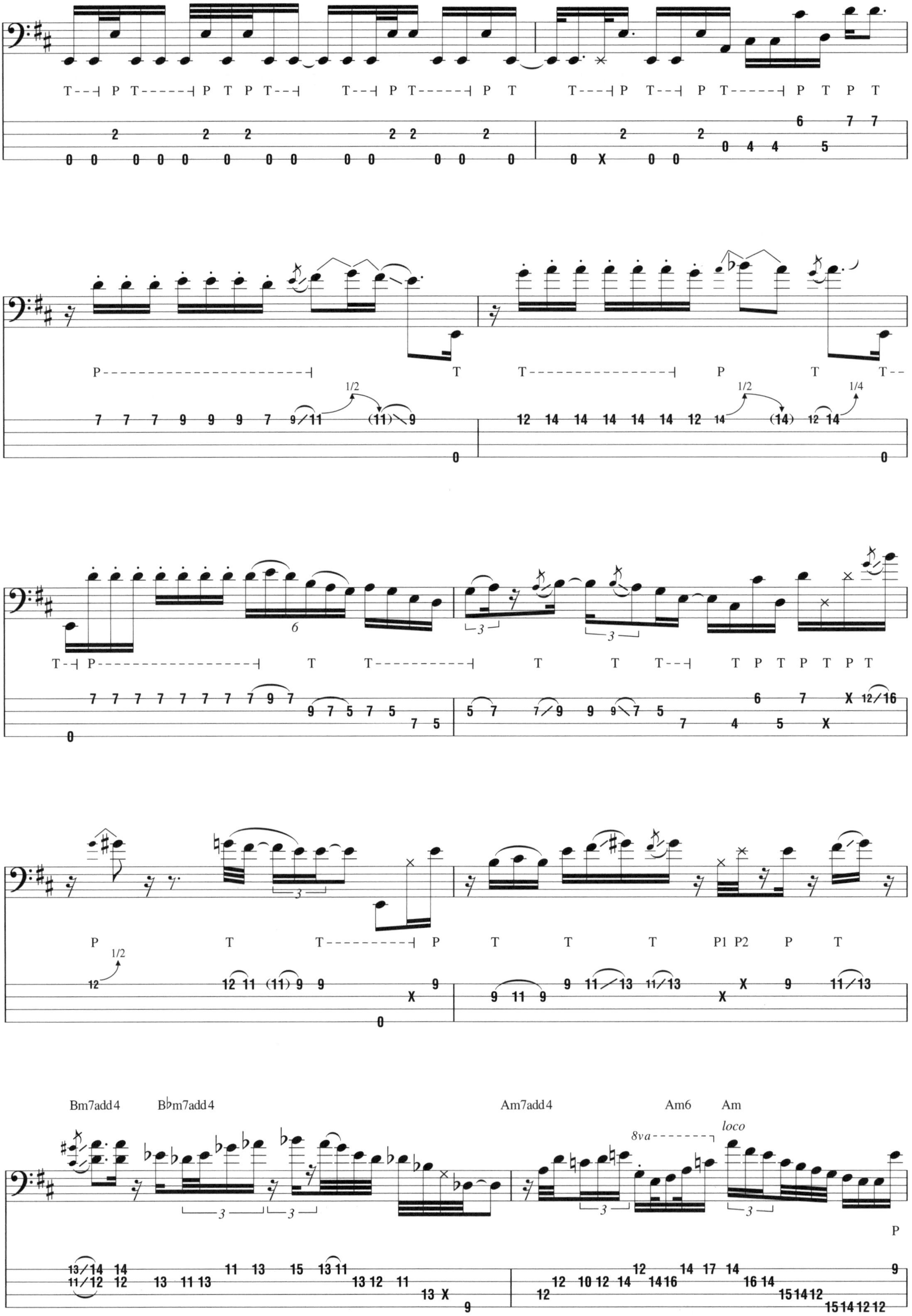
Bm7add4
B♭m7add4
Am7add4
Am6
Am
8va
loco

E
Bm7add4 B♭m7add4
Am6
Am
I
C7♯9
E♭
F
C7♯9
E♭
F
C7♯9

E♭
F
C7♯9
8va
loco
T
T T T T T
8va
loco
A5 B♭5 B5
T
H.H.
T
P T T P
*Hypothetical fret location.
J
E7sus4
E6/9
E7sus4
E6/9
8va
loco
P.M.
T P P P
E7sus4
E6/9
Am7add6
E7sus4
E6/9
P P P P T
T T
E7sus4
E6/9
E7sus4
E6/9
Am7add6
T T T P P P
P P T

K
N.C. (E)
L
E
8va
loco
1/4

8va
loco

from - *Free*

Strum

By Marcus Miller

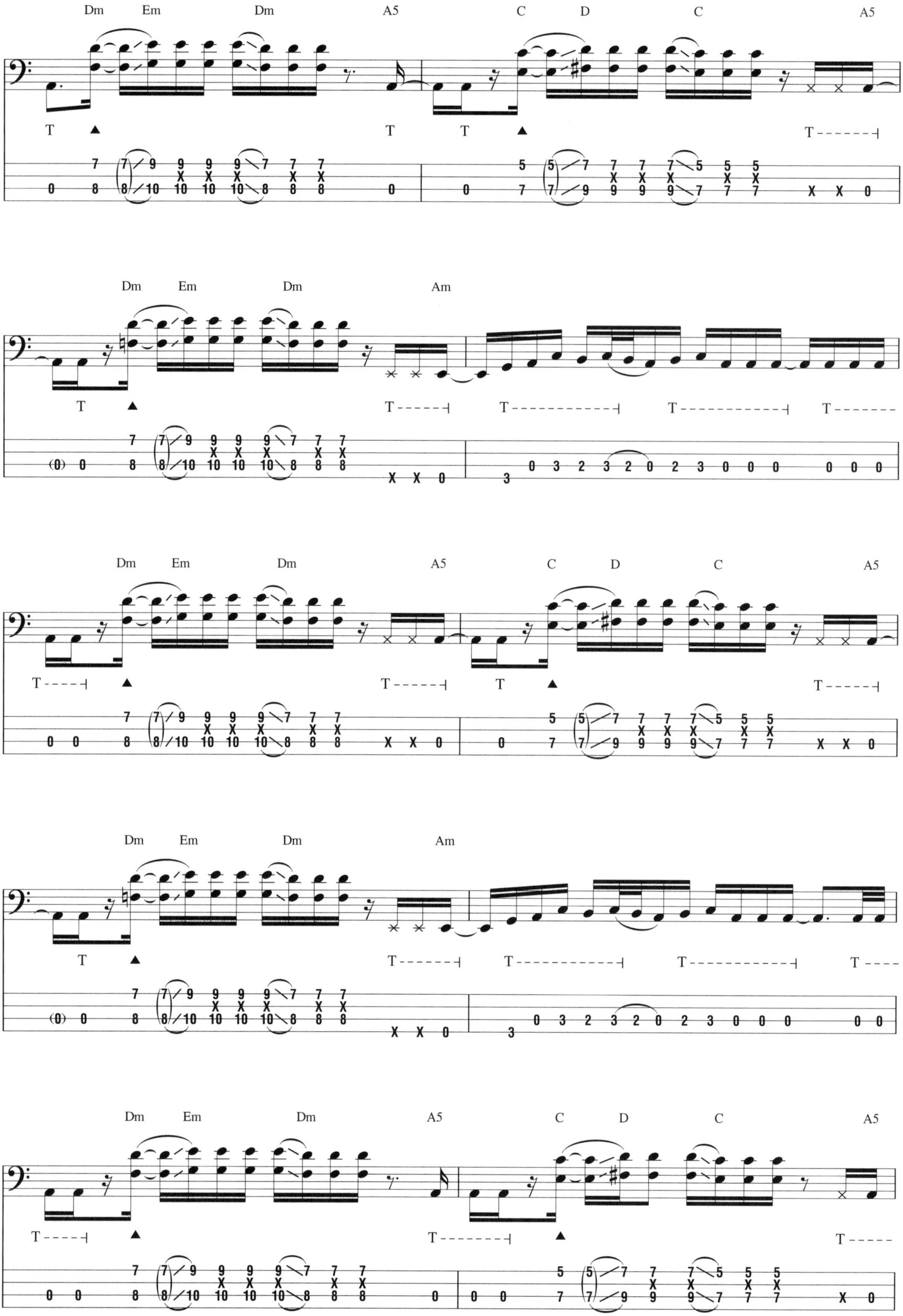
Dm Em Dm A5 C D C A5
Dm Em Dm Am
Dm Em Dm A5 C D C A5
Dm Em Dm Am
Dm Em Dm A5 C D C A5

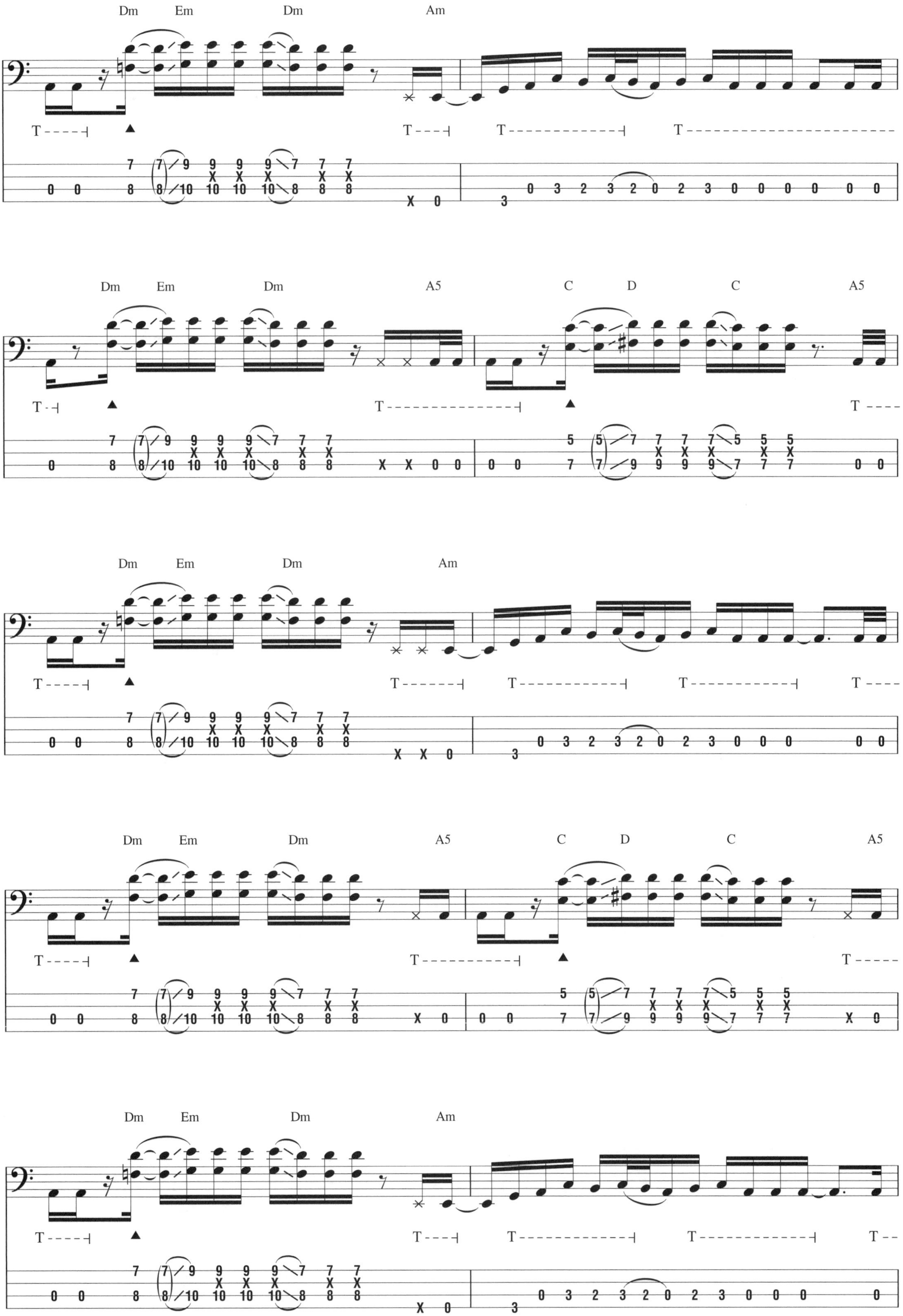
Dm Em Dm Am
Dm Em Dm A5 C D C A5
Dm Em Dm Am
Dm Em Dm A5 C D C A5
Dm Em Dm Am

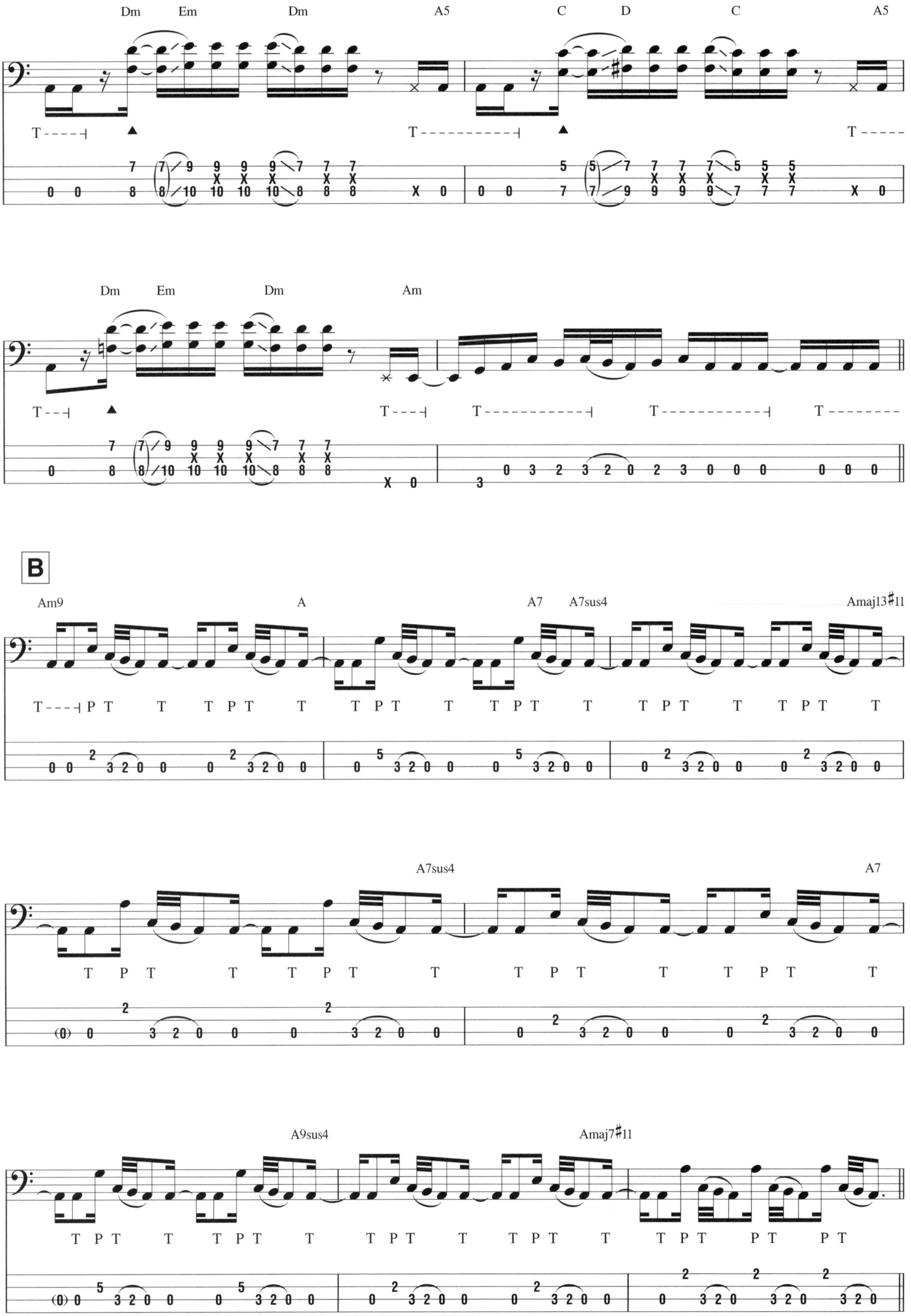
Dm Em Dm A5 C D C A5
Dm Em Dm Am
B
Am9 A A7 A7sus4 Amaj13♯11
A7sus4 A7
A9sus4 Amaj7♯11

C
A5 Dm Em Dm A5 C D C A5
Dm Em Dm Am
Dm Em Dm A5 C D C A5
Dm Em Dm Am
Dm Em Dm A5 C D C A5

Dm Em Dm Am
Dm Em Dm A5 C D C A5
Dm Em Dm Am
Dm Em Dm A5 C D C A5
Dm Em Dm A5

Dm Em Dm A5 C D C A5
Dm Em Dm Am
Dm Em Dm A5 C D C A5
Dm Em Dm Am
D
Am9 A A7sus4

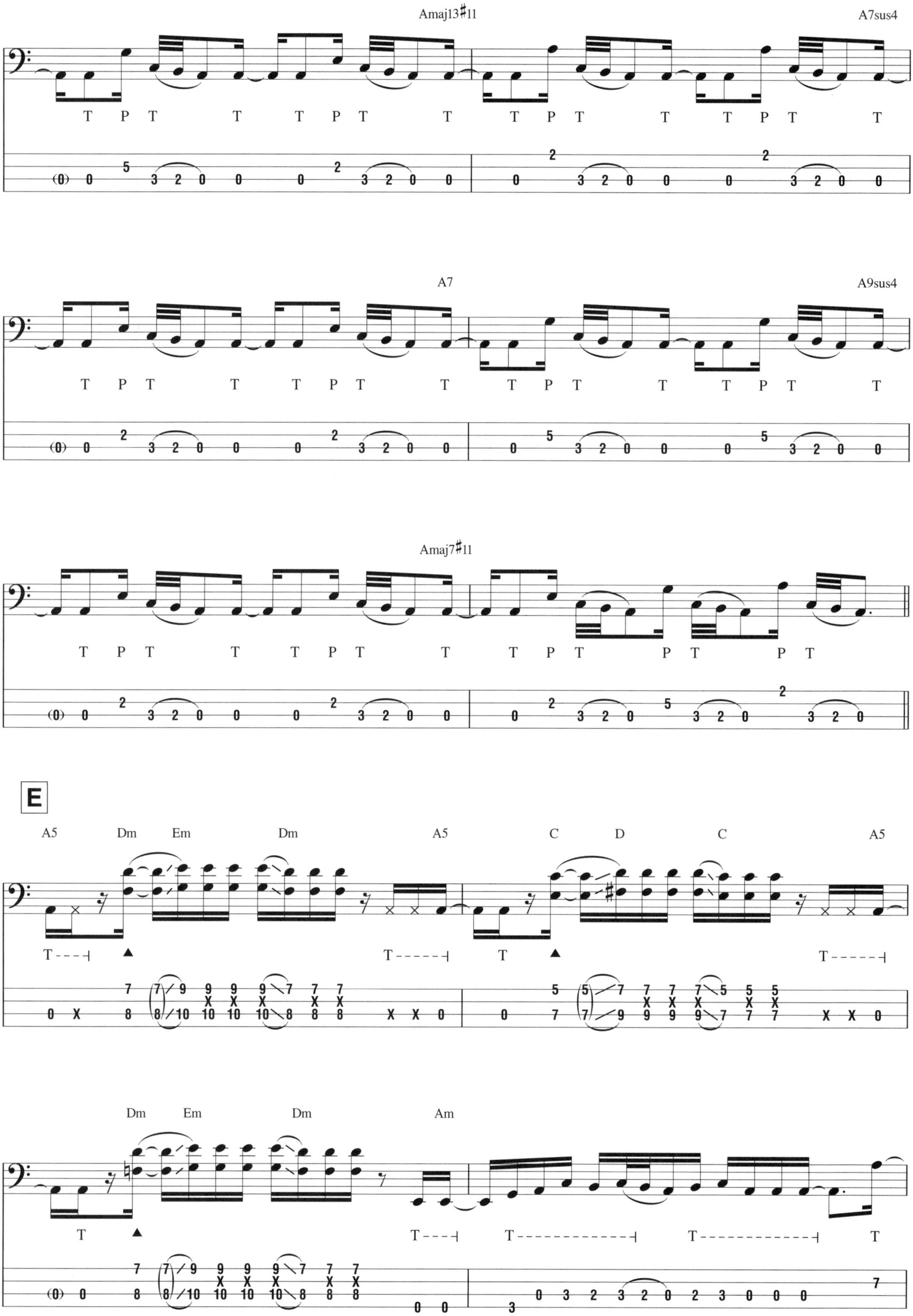
Amaj13♯11
A7sus4
A7
A9sus4
Amaj7♯11
E
A5
Dm
Em
Dm
A5
C
D
C
A5
Dm
Em
Dm
Am

Dm Em Dm A5 C D C A5
Dm Em Dm Am
F
Dm A Dm F♯
A Dm
steady gliss.
G
A5 Dm Em Dm A5 C D C A5

Dm Em Dm Am
Dm Em Dm A5 C D C A5
Dm Em Dm Am
Dm Em Dm A5 C D C A5
Dm Em Dm Am A

*P2 = Pluck w/ 2nd finger
P1 = Pluck w/ index finger

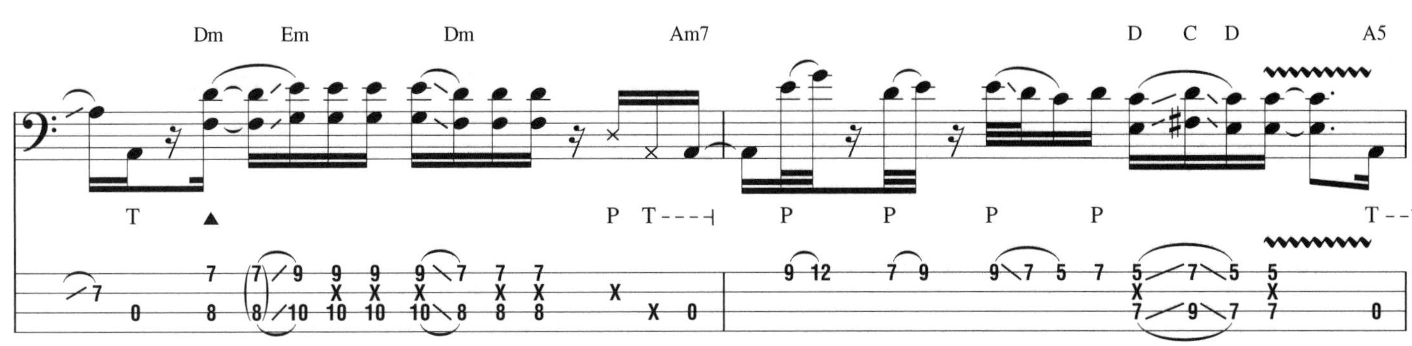

Dm Em Dm Am
Dm Em Dm A5 C D C A5
Dm Em Dm Am
Dm Em Dm A5 C5 D C A5
Dm Em Dm Am

from M^2

3 Deuces

By Marcus Miller

B
E♭m7
Dm7
A7♭9♯5
N.C.
P.M.
P.M.
P.M.
A7♭9♯5
Dm9
E♭7
Dm9
A7♭9♯5
Dm9
P.M.
Cm9
Dm7
A7♭9♯5
Dm9
E♭7
Dm9
P.M.

A7♭9♯5
Dm9
E♭maj7
Dm7
A7♭9♯5
Dm9
P.M.
E♭7
Dm9
A7♭9♯5
Dm9
C9(no3rd)
Dm
P.M.
A7♭9♯5
Dm9
E♭7
Dm9
A7♭9♯5
Dm9
P.M.
C
C9(no3rd)
Dm
A7♭9♯5
Dm9
E♭7
Dm9
P.M.
A7♭9♯5
Dm9
C9(no3rd)
Dm
A7♭9♯5
Dm9
1/4

E♭7 Dm9 A7♭9♯5 Dm9 C9(no3rd) Dm
A7♭9♯5 Dm9 E♭7 Dm9 A7♭9♯5 Dm9
C9(no3rd) Dm A7♭9♯5 Dm9 E♭7 Dm9
A7♭9♯5 Dm9 C9(no3rd) Dm A7♭9♯5 Dm9
E♭7 Dm9 A7♭9♯5 Dm9 C9(no3rd) Dm
1/4
8va

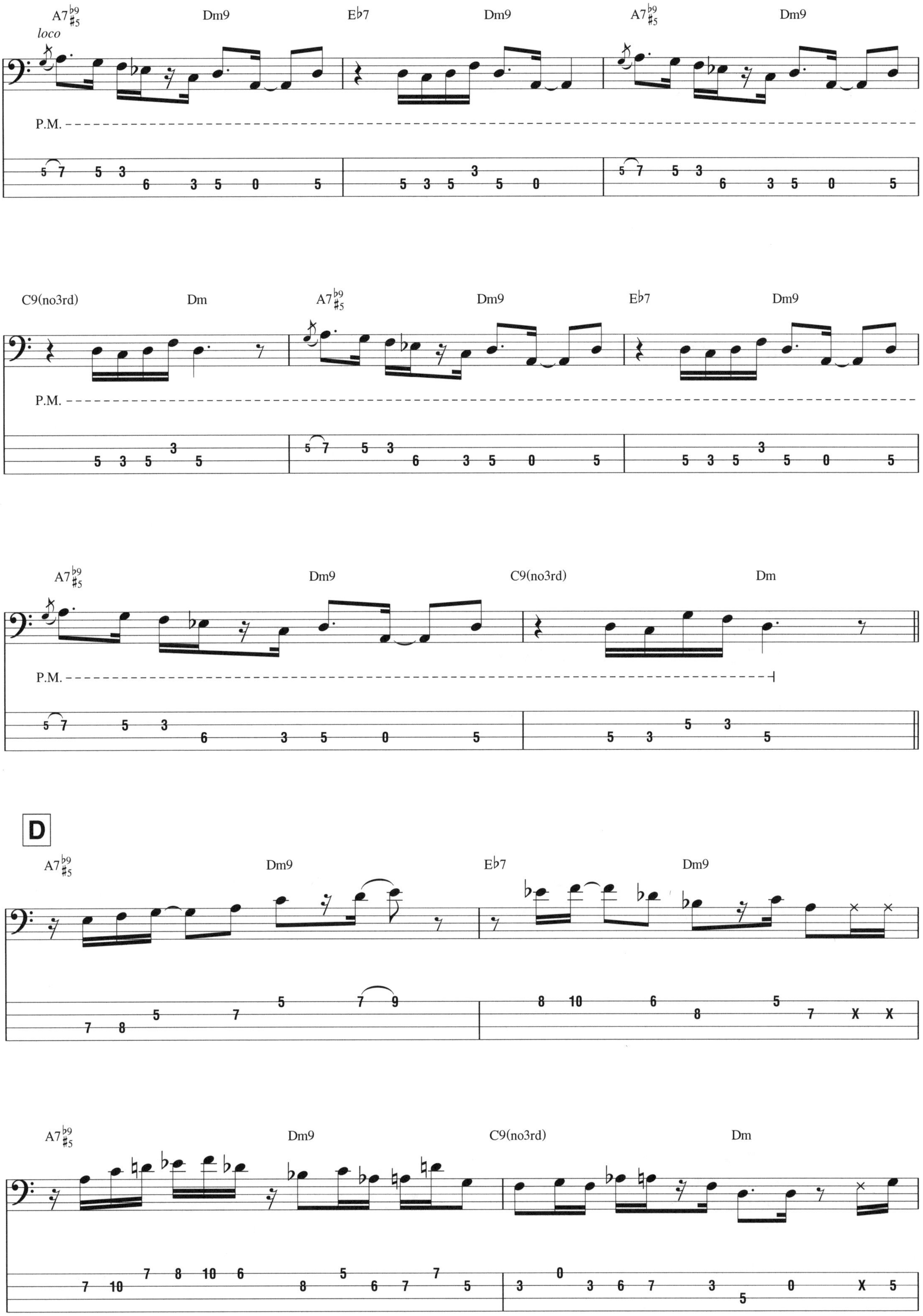
A7♭9♯5
loco
Dm9
E♭7
Dm9
A7♭9♯5
Dm9
P.M.
C9(no3rd)
Dm
A7♭9♯5
Dm9
E♭7
Dm9
P.M.
A7♭9♯5
Dm9
C9(no3rd)
Dm
P.M.
D
A7♭9♯5
Dm9
E♭7
Dm9
A7♭9♯5
Dm9
C9(no3rd)
Dm

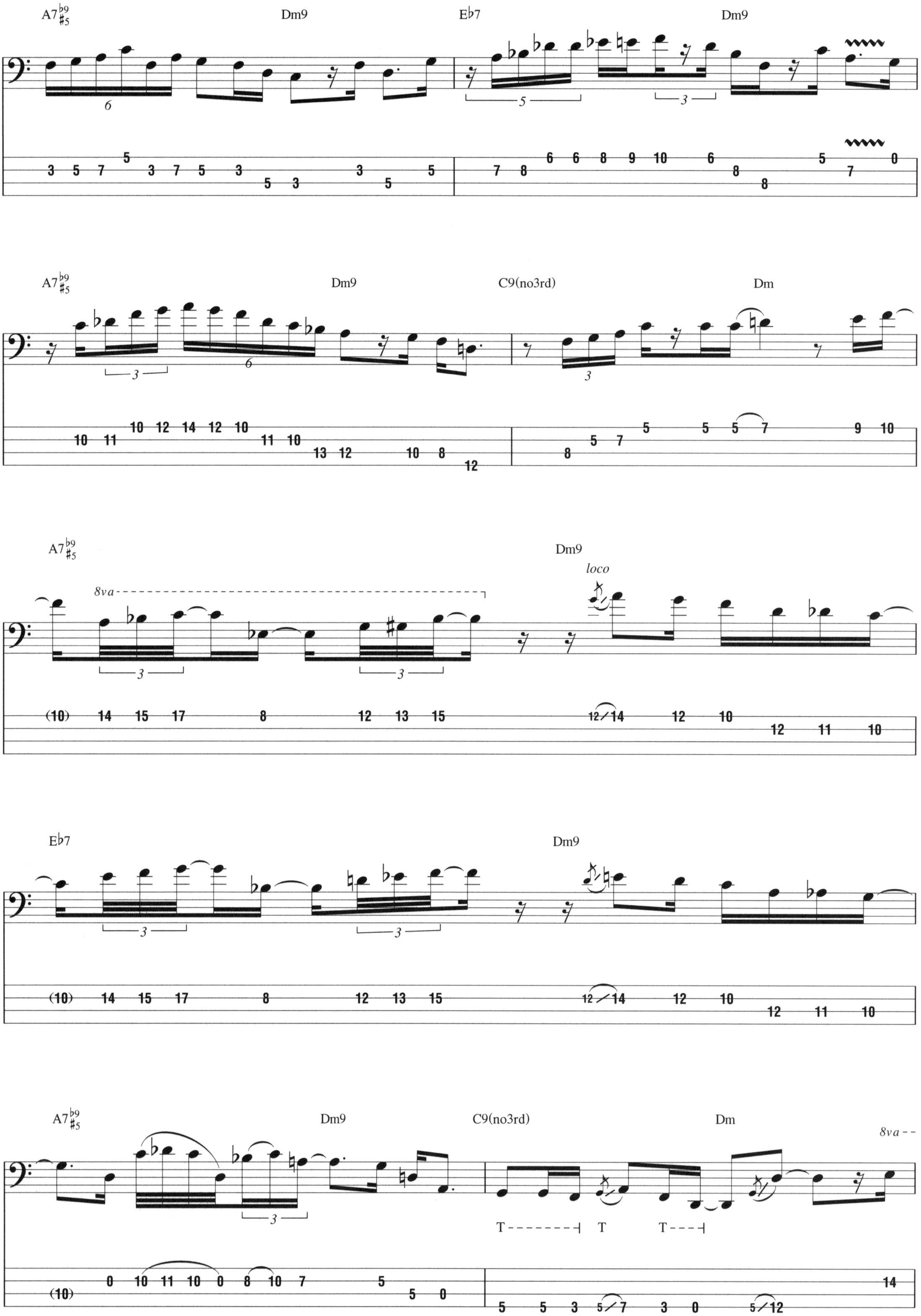
A7♭9♯5
Dm9
E♭7
Dm9
A7♭9♯5
Dm9
C9(no3rd)
Dm
A7♭9♯5
8va
Dm9
loco
E♭7
Dm9
A7♭9♯5
Dm9
C9(no3rd)
Dm
8va

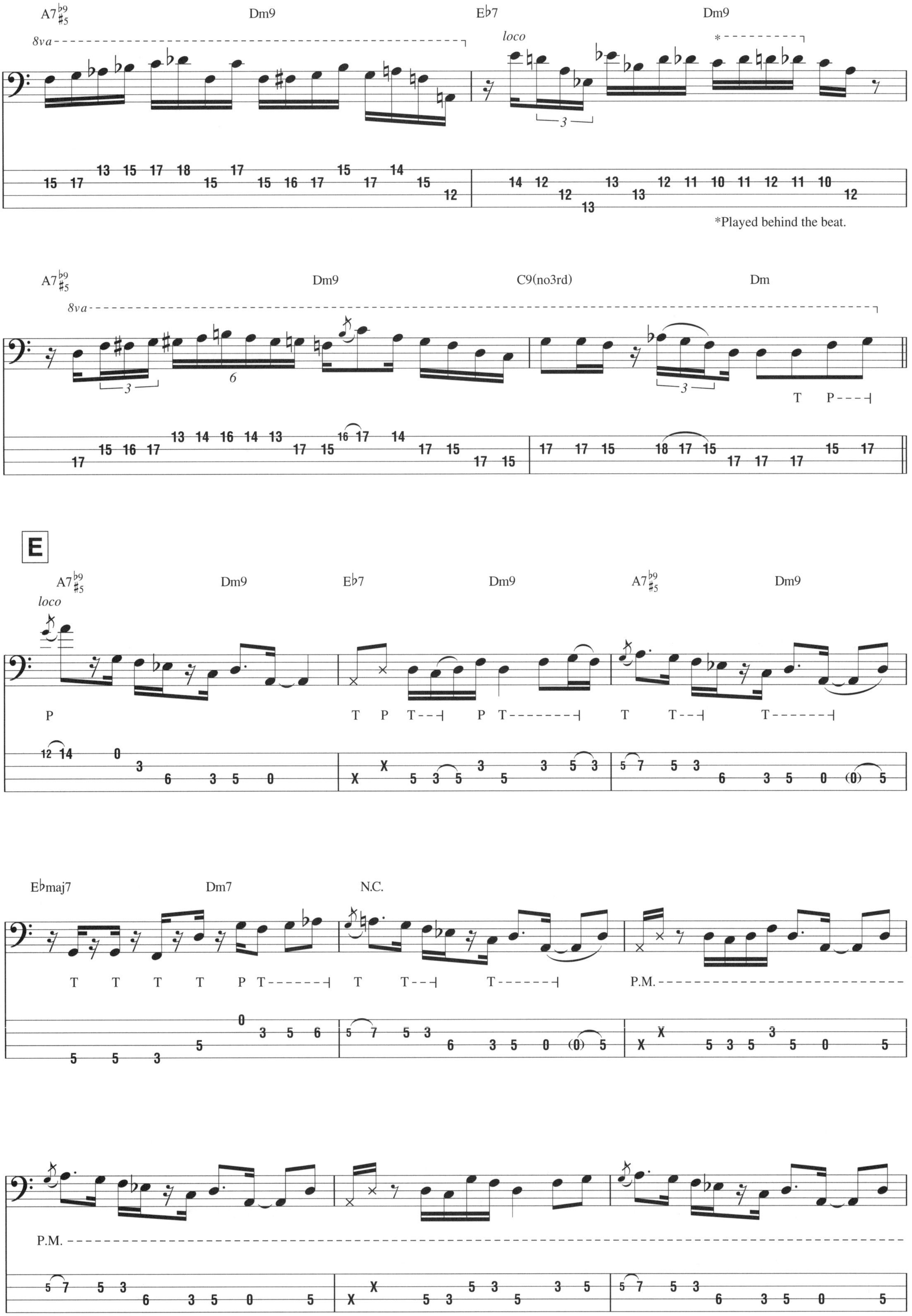
A7♭9♯5
Dm9
E♭7
Dm9
8va
loco
*Played behind the beat.
A7♭9♯5
Dm9
C9(no3rd)
Dm
E
A7♭9♯5
Dm9
E♭7
Dm9
A7♭9♯5
Dm9
loco
E♭maj7
Dm7
N.C.
P.M.

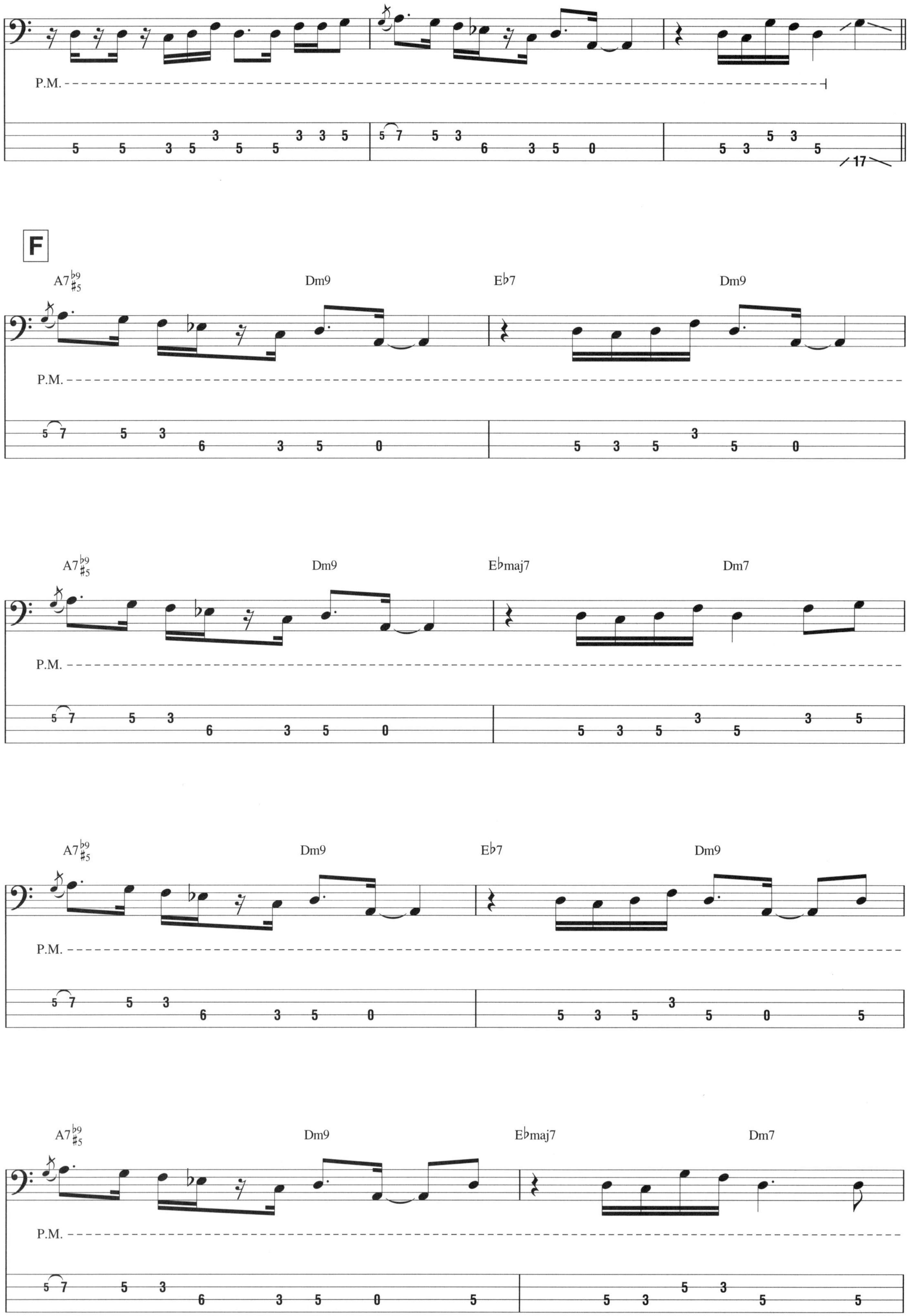
P.M.
F
A7♭9♯5
Dm9
E♭7
Dm9
P.M.
A7♭9♯5
Dm9
E♭maj7
Dm7
P.M.
A7♭9♯5
Dm9
E♭7
Dm9
P.M.
A7♭9♯5
Dm9
E♭maj7
Dm7
P.M.

A7♭9♯5
Dm9
E♭7
Dm9
P.M.
A7♭9♯5
Dm9
E♭maj7
Dm7
A7♭9♯5
Dm9
E♭7
Dm9
A7♭9♯5
Dm9
E♭maj7
Dm7
1/4
A7♭9♯5
Dm9
E♭7
Dm9

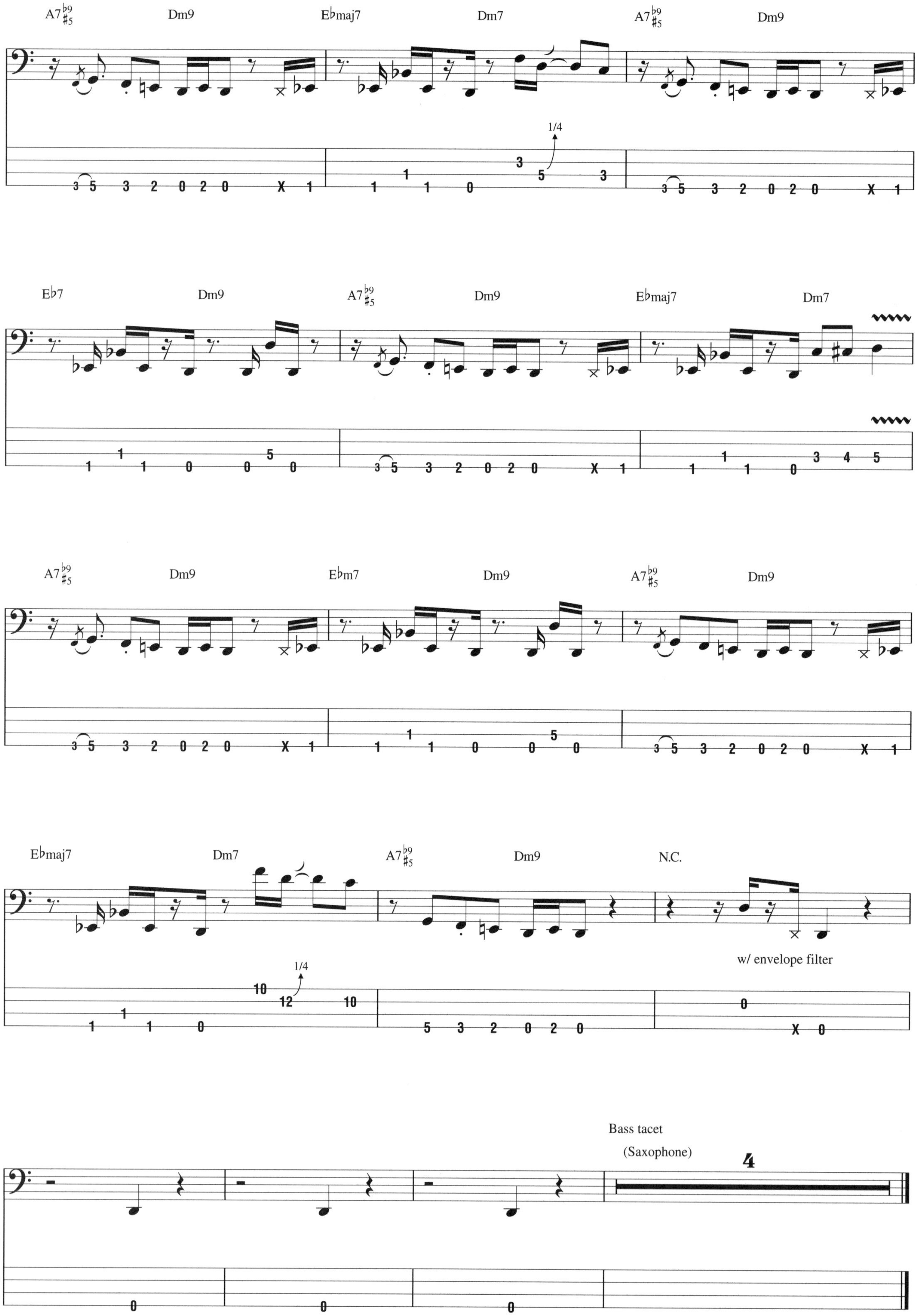
A7♭9♯5
Dm9
E♭maj7
Dm7
E♭7
E♭m7
N.C.
1/4
w/ envelope filter
Bass tacet
(Saxophone)
4

from Miles Davis - *Tutu*

Tutu

By Marcus Miller

Bass 1: Drop D tuning:
(low to high) D-A-D-G

1/4
P
P
Gm11
Gm6/9
Gmaj7sus4♯11
Gm♭6
E5add♭2
A5add♭2
D5add♭2
B(♭5)add♭2
Dm6/9
Gm

C
Gm11
Gm6/9
Gmaj7sus4♯11
Gm♭6
Gm11

Gm6/9
Gmaj7sus4#11
Gm♭6
P
E5add♭2 A5add♭2 D5add♭2 B(♭5)add♭2 Dm6/9
Gm
1/4
P
15ma
Harm.
Pitch: G D
D A
P
P

15ma
Harm.
Pitch: G D
D A
P
*
-1
slack
*Tune down tuning peg.
loco
1/4
P
P T
P

D
Gm11
Gm6/9
Gmaj7sus4♯11
Gm♭6
Gm11
Gm6/9
Gmaj7sus4♯11
Gm♭6

E5add♭2 A5add♭2 D5add♭2 B(♭5)add♭2 Dm6/9
Gm
E
Gm11
Gm6/9
Gmaj7sus4♯11

Gm♭6
Gm11
P P
Gm6/9
Gmaj7sus4♯11
Gm♭6
1/4
P
Gm11
Gm6/9
Gmaj7sus4♯11
1/4
P T
P

Gm♭6
Gm
P
P
X
1/4
Begin fade
Fade out
1/4
P

from - *Free*

What Is Hip

Words and Music by Stephen Kupka, Emilio Castillo and David Garibaldi

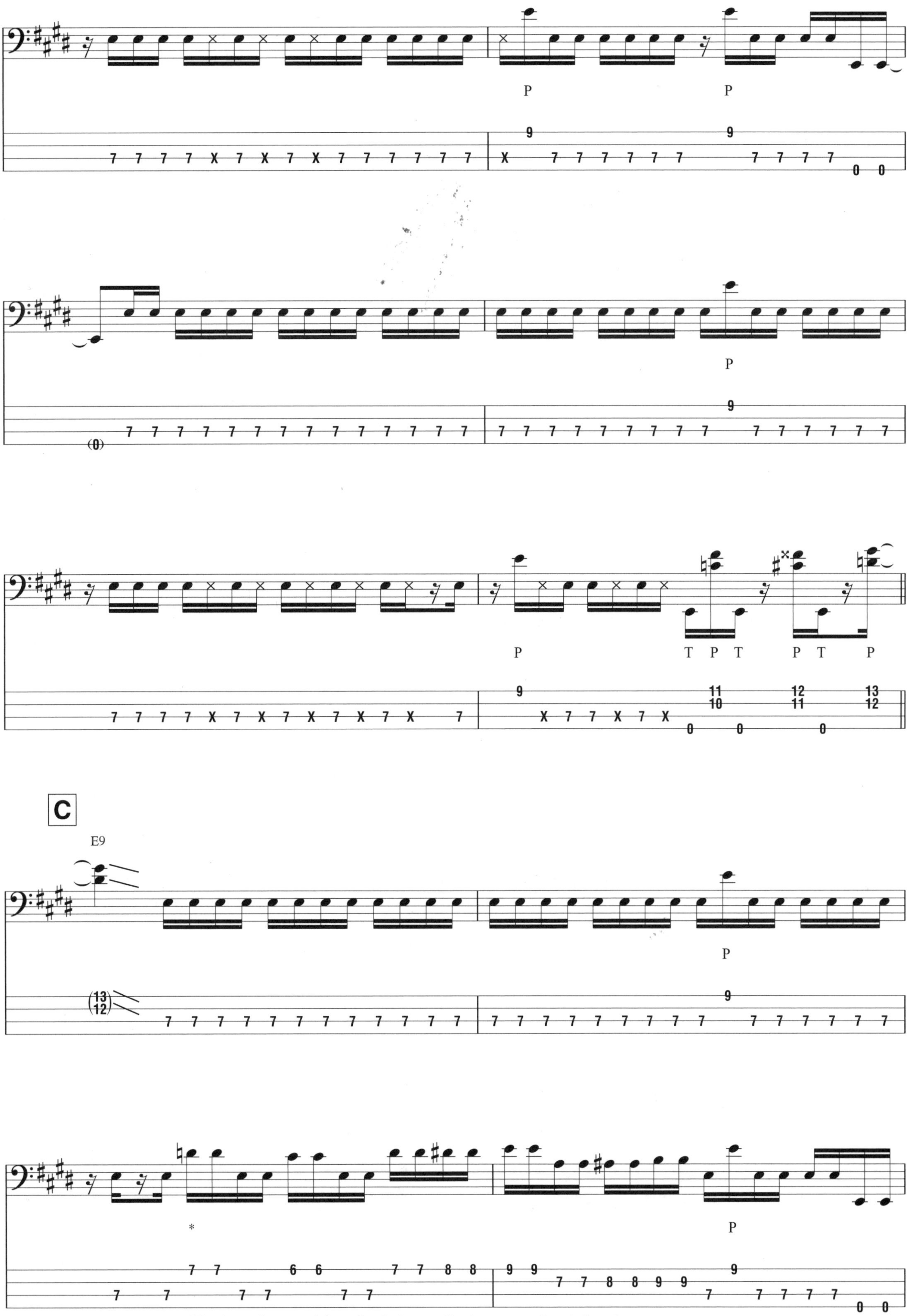

*Continue using up-and-down thumb slaps on all strings except where indicated.

P
P
C
E9
P
B7
E7
P
F#7
G

E9
D
E9

P
P
P
C
E9
T
T
B7
E7

F♯7
G
P P P P
T P P P P
T P P P P
N.C.
T P P P P
steady gliss.
E
Am
T
E7
Am
T
E7

Am
E7
T
Am
B
C
E9
T
F
E9
P
T P T P T P
steady gliss.
w/ fingers

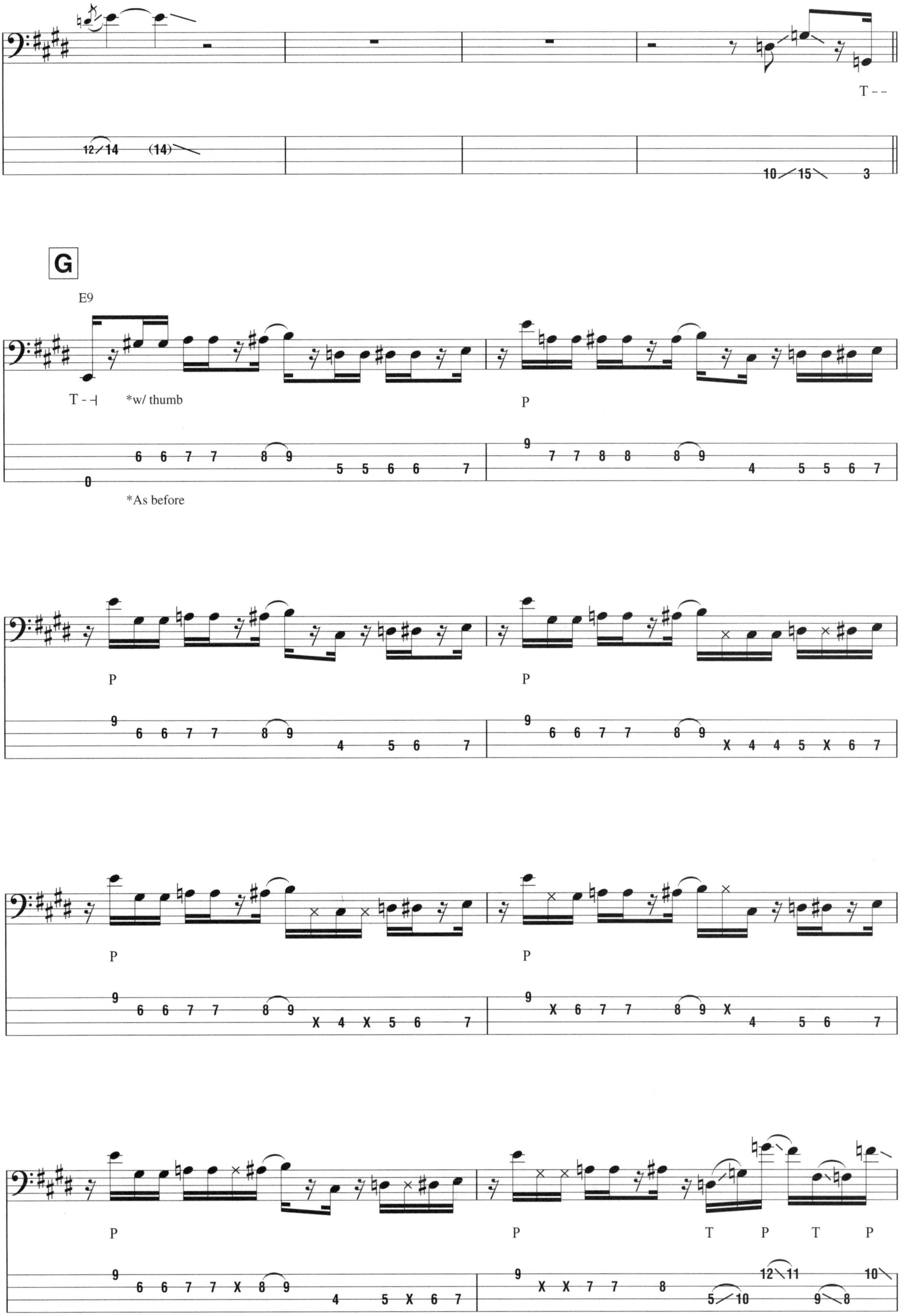
T - -
G
E9
T - ˧
*w/ thumb
*As before
P
P
P
P
P
P
P
T
P
T
P

5
H
E9

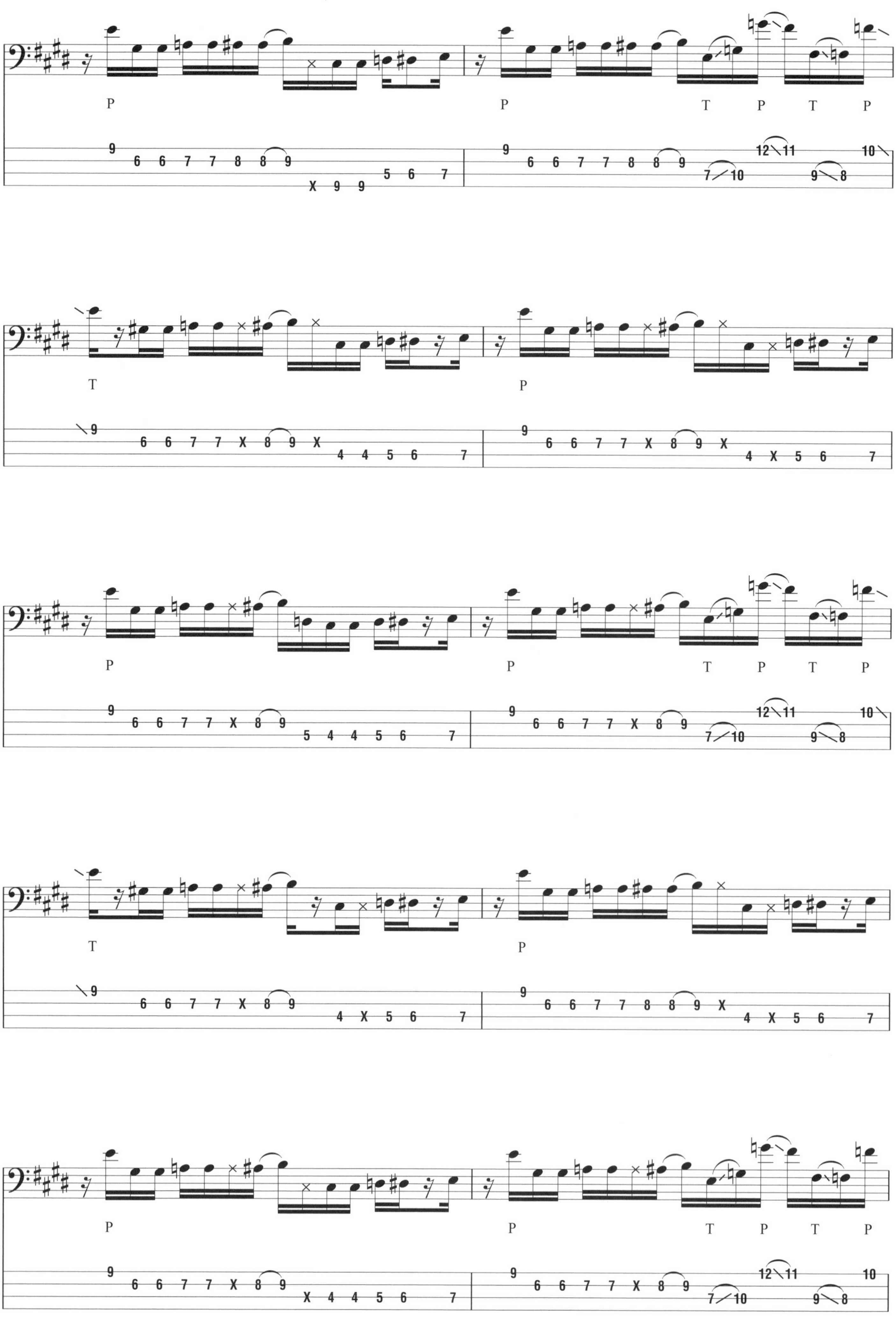

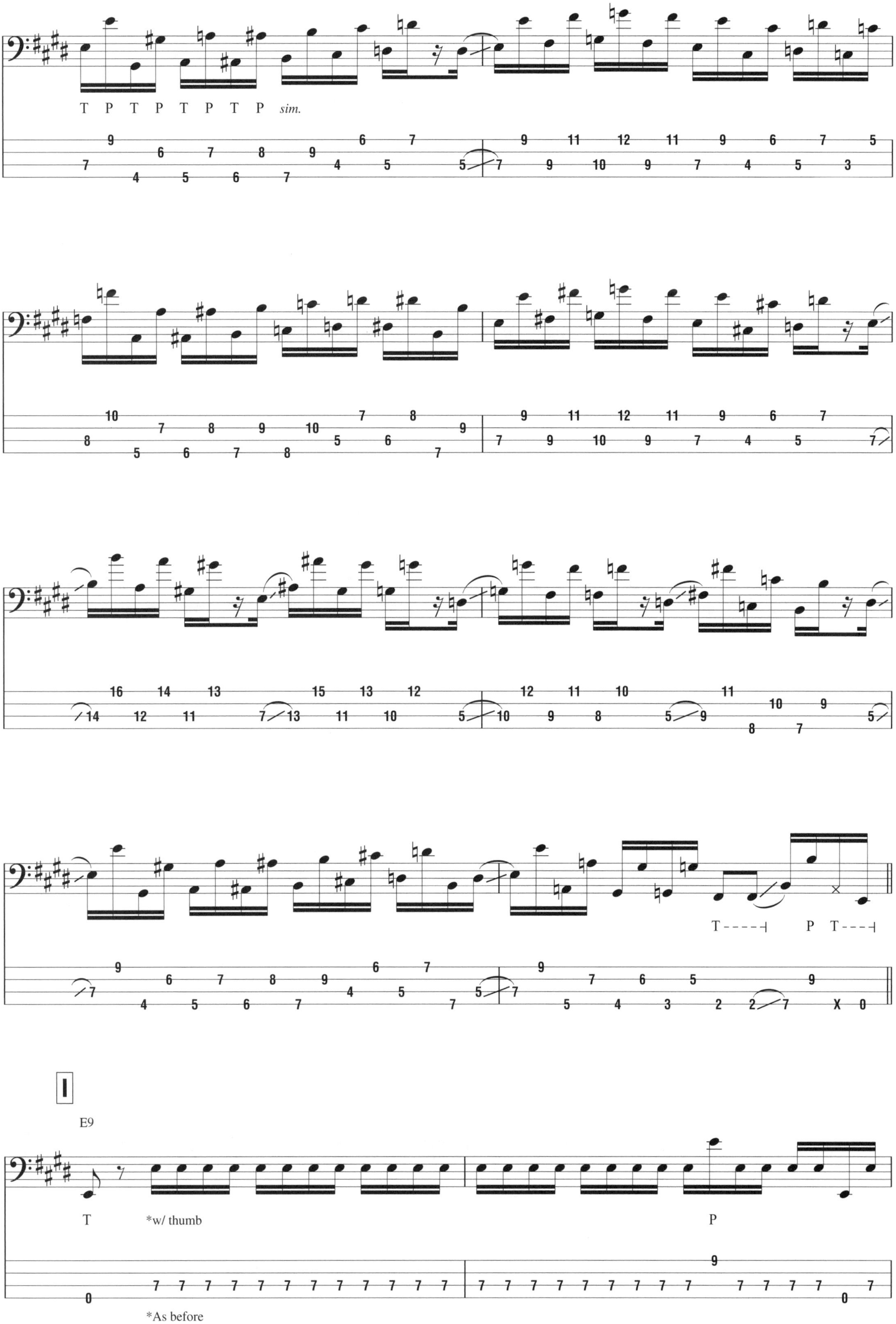
T P T P T P T P sim.
T----
P T----
I
E9
T
*w/ thumb
P
*As before

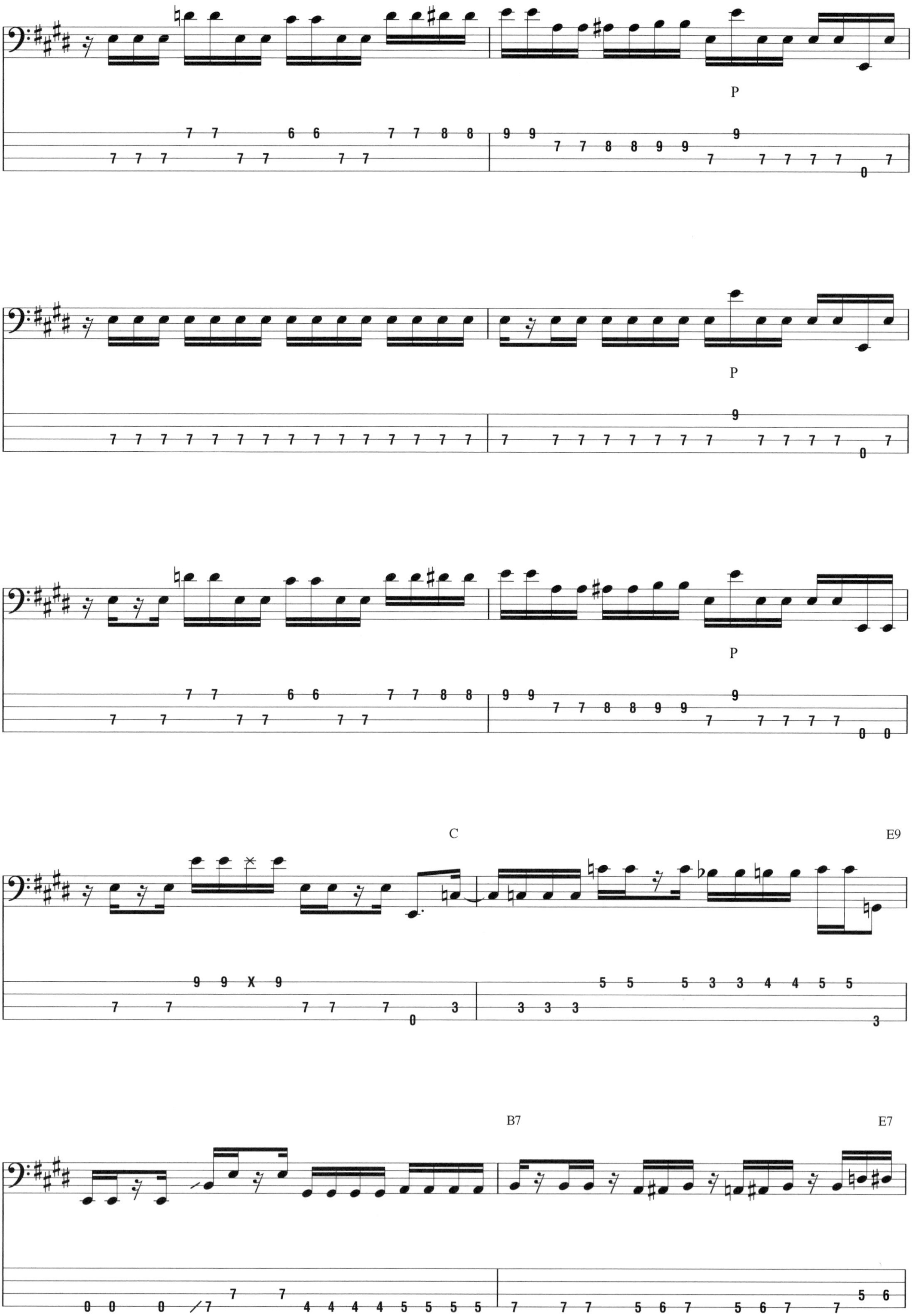
P
P
P
C
E9
B7
E7

F♯7
G
T P P P P
T P P P P
Em9
T P P P P
T P P P P T T T T
J
Em9
C♯m9
T T T T
Em9
T T T T

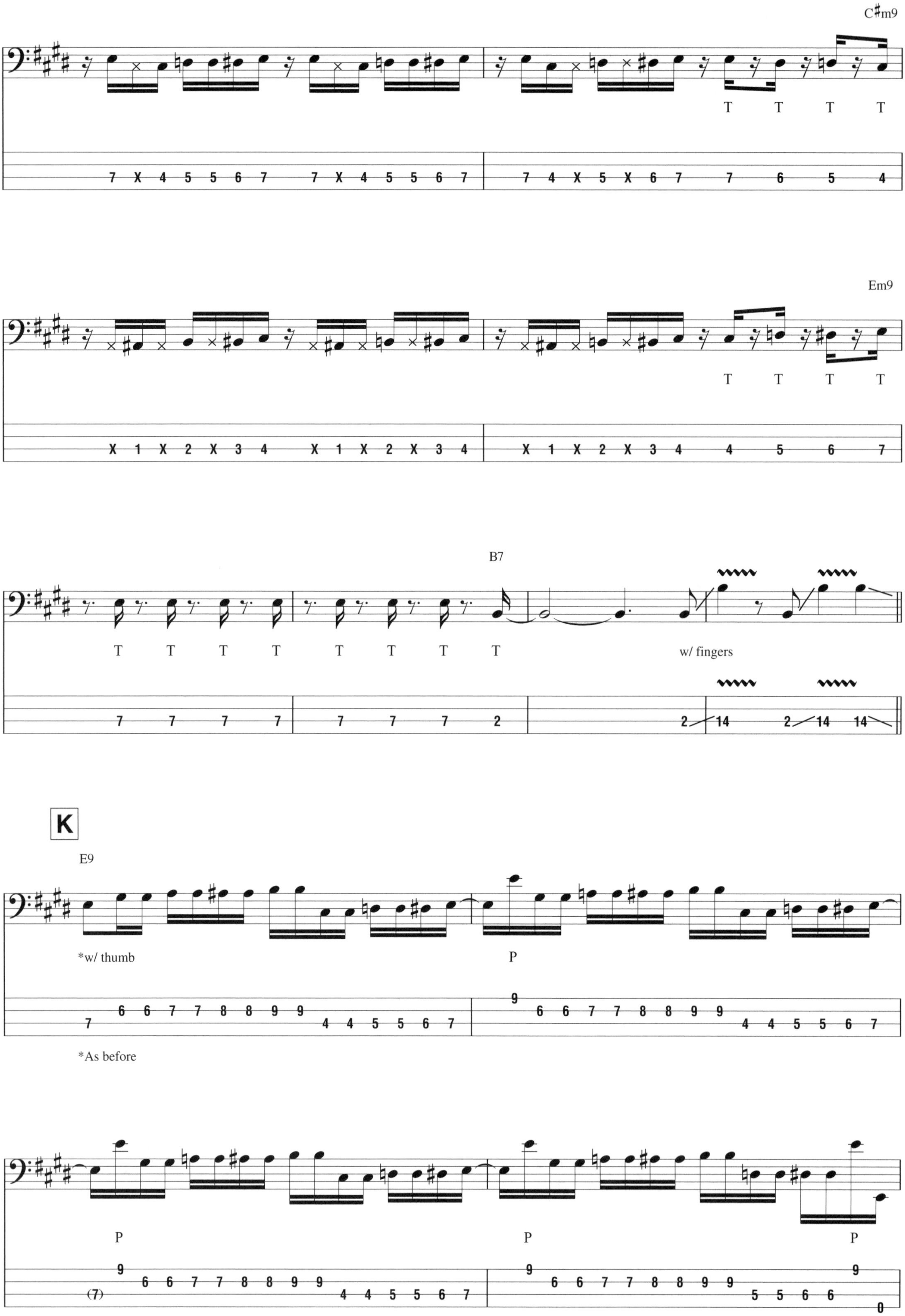
C♯m9
T T T T
Em9
T T T T
B7
T T T T T T T T
w/ fingers
K
E9
*w/ thumb
P
*As before
P
P
P

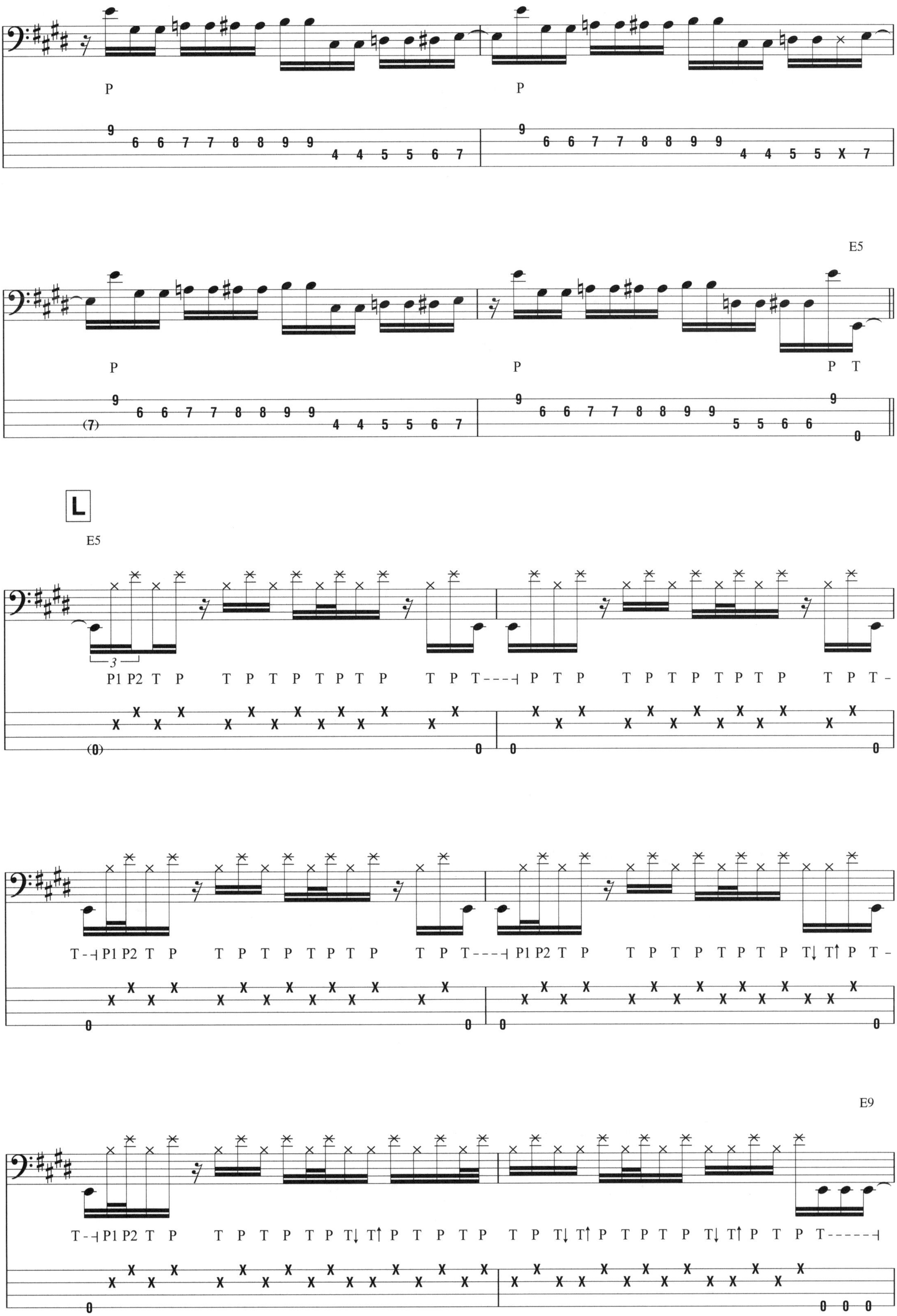
E5
L
E5
E9

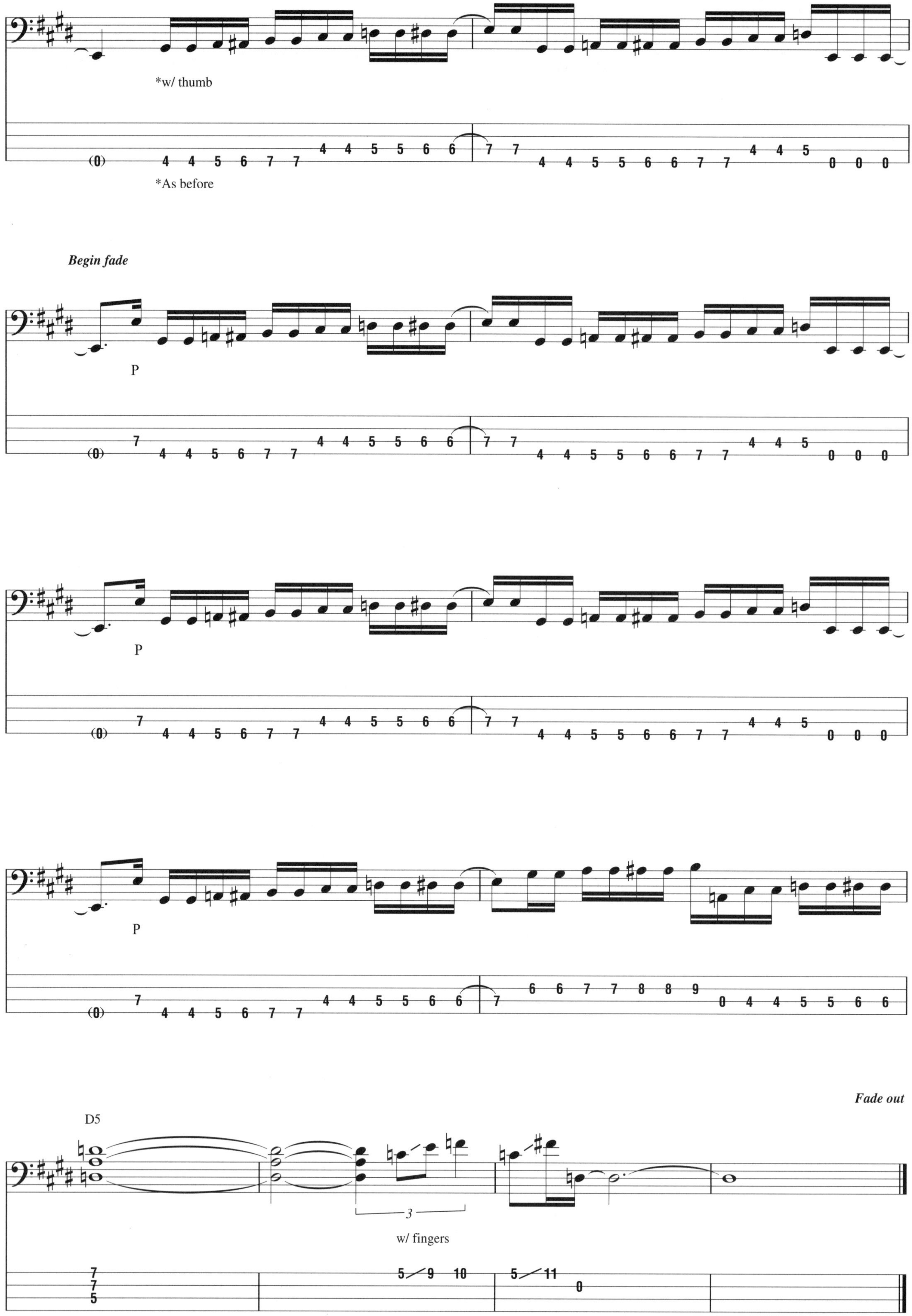
*w/ thumb
*As before
Begin fade
P
P
P
D5
w/ fingers
Fade out

Bass Notation Legend

Bass music can be notated two different ways: on a *musical staff*, and in *tablature*.

THE MUSICAL STAFF shows pitches and rhythms and is divided by bar lines into measures. Pitches are named after the first seven letters of the alphabet.

TABLATURE graphically represents the bass fingerboard. Each horizontal line represents a string, and each number represents a fret.

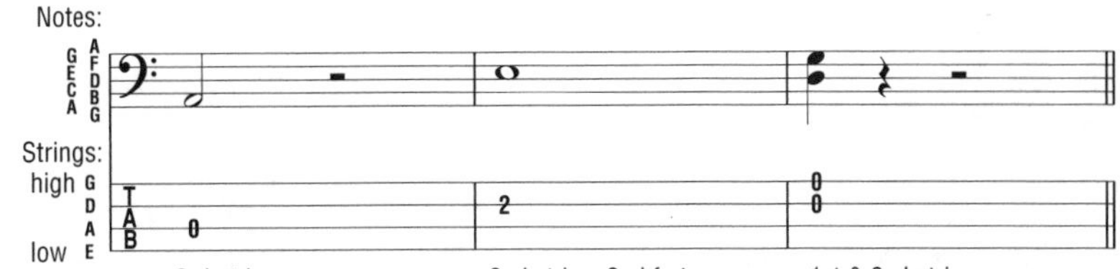

3rd string, open — 2nd string, 2nd fret — 1st & 2nd strings open, played together

HAMMER-ON: Strike the first (lower) note with one finger, then sound the higher note (on the same string) with another finger by fretting it without picking.

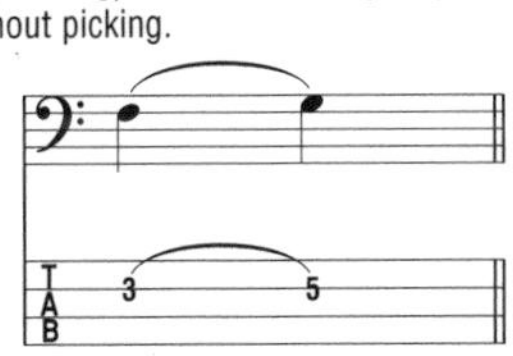

PULL-OFF: Place both fingers on the notes to be sounded. Strike the first note and without picking, pull the finger off to sound the second (lower) note.

LEGATO SLIDE: Strike the first note and then slide the same fret-hand finger up or down to the second note. The second note is not struck.

SHIFT SLIDE: Same as legato slide, except the second note is struck.

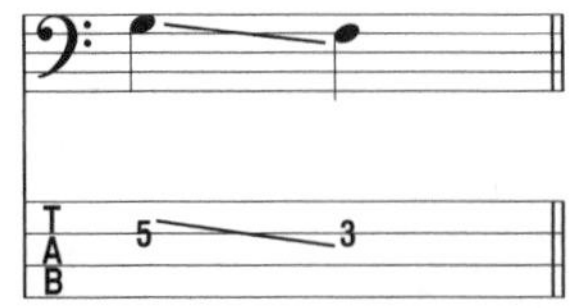

TRILL: Very rapidly alternate between the notes indicated by continuously hammering on and pulling off.

TREMOLO PICKING: The note is picked as rapidly and continuously as possible.

VIBRATO: The string is vibrated by rapidly bending and releasing the note with the fretting hand.

SHAKE: Using one finger, rapidly alternate between two notes on one string by sliding either a half-step above or below.

NATURAL HARMONIC: Strike the note while the fret hand lightly touches the string directly over the fret indicated.

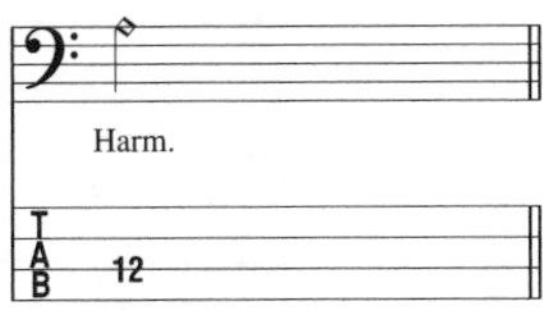

MUFFLED STRINGS: A percussive sound is produced by laying the fret hand across the string(s) without depressing them and striking them with the pick hand.

BEND: Strike the note and bend up the interval shown.

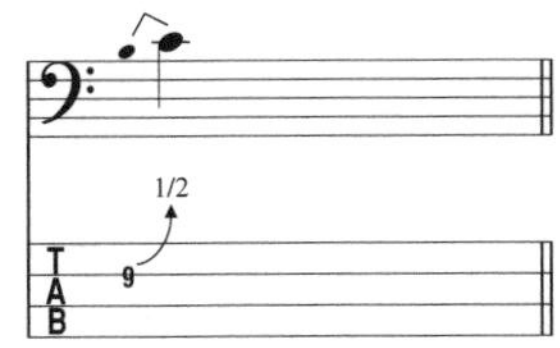

BEND AND RELEASE: Strike the note and bend up as indicated, then release back to the original note. Only the first note is struck.

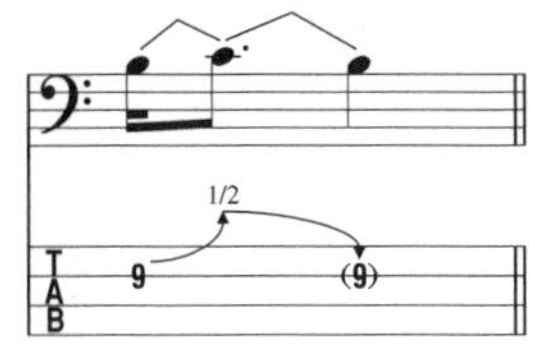

RIGHT-HAND TAP: Hammer ("tap") the fret indicated with the "pick-hand" index or middle finger and pull off to the note fretted by the fret hand.

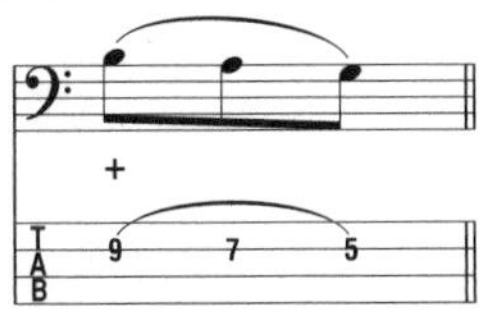

LEFT-HAND TAP: Hammer ("tap") the fret indicated with the "fret-hand" index or middle finger.

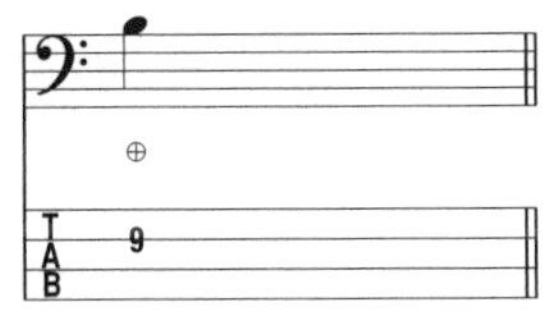

SLAP: Strike ("slap") string with right-hand thumb.

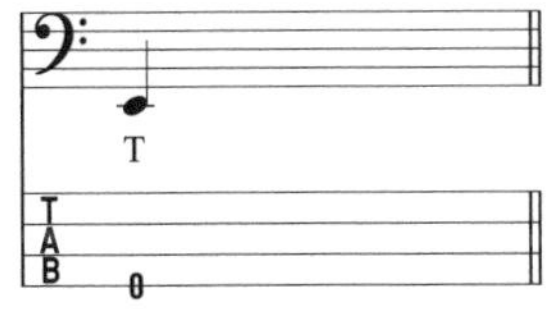

POP: Snap ("pop") string with right-hand index or middle finger.

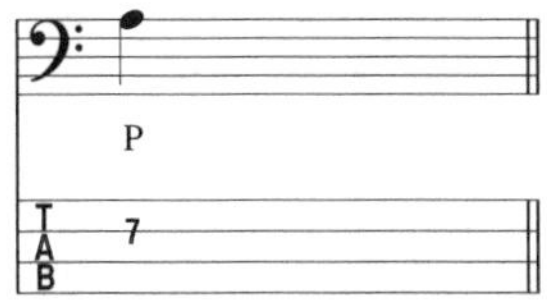

Additional Musical Definitions

 *(accent)* • Accentuate note (play it louder).

 *(accent)* • Accentuate note with great intensity.

 *(staccato)* • Play the note short.

⊓ • Downstroke

V • Upstroke

D.S. al Coda • Go back to the sign (𝄋), then play until the measure marked "***To Coda***," then skip to the section labelled "**Coda.**"

D.C. al Fine • Go back to the beginning of the song and play until the measure marked "***Fine***" (end).

Bass Fig. • Label used to recall a recurring pattern.

Fill • Label used to identify a brief melodic figure which is to be inserted into the arrangement.

tacet • Instrument is silent (drops out).

 • Repeat measures between signs.

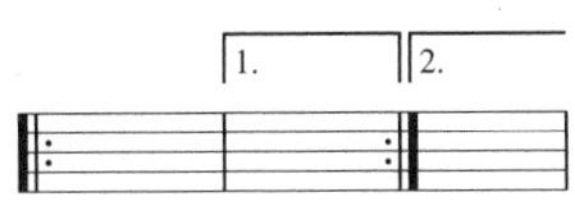

• When a repeated section has different endings, play the first ending only the first time and the second ending only the second time.

NOTE: Tablature numbers in parentheses mean:

1. The note is being sustained over a system (note in standard notation is tied), or
2. The note is sustained, but a new articulation (such as a hammer-on, pull-off, slide or vibrato) begins, or
3. The note is a barely audible "ghost" note (note in standard notation is also in parentheses).

BASS RECORDED VERSIONS

Bass Recorded Versions® feature authentic transcriptions written in standard notation and tablature for bass guitar. This series features complete bass lines from the classics to contemporary superstars.

25 All-Time Rock Bass Classics
00690445 / $14.95

25 Essential Rock Bass Classics
00690210 / $15.95

Aerosmith Bass Collection
00690413 / $17.95

Best of Victor Bailey
00690718 / $19.95

Bass Tab 1990-1999
00690400 / $16.95

Bass Tab 1999-2000
00690404 / $14.95

Bass Tab White Pages
00690508 / $29.95

The Beatles Bass Lines
00690170 / $14.95

The Beatles 1962-1966
00690556 / $18.99

The Beatles 1967-1970
00690557 / $18.99

Best Bass Rock Hits
00694803 / $12.95

Black Sabbath – We Sold Our Soul For Rock 'N' Roll
00660116 / $17.95

The Best of Blink 182
00690549 / $18.95

Blues Bass Classics
00690291 / $14.95

Boston Bass Collection
00690935 / $19.95

Chart Hits for Bass
00690729 / $14.95

The Best of Eric Clapton
00660187 / $19.95

Stanley Clarke Collection
00672307 / $19.95

Funk Bass Bible
00690744 / $19.95

Hard Rock Bass Bible
00690746 / $17.95

Jimi Hendrix – Are You Experienced?
00690371 / $17.95

The Buddy Holly Bass Book
00660132 / $12.95

Incubus – Morning View
00690639 / $17.95

Iron Maiden Bass Anthology
00690867 / $22.99

Best of Kiss for Bass
00690080 / $19.95

Bob Marley Bass Collection
00690568 / $19.95

Best of Marcus Miller
00690811 / $19.99

Motown Bass Classics
00690253 / $14.95

Mudvayne – Lost & Found
00690798 / $19.95

Nirvana Bass Collection
00690066 / $19.95

No Doubt – Tragic Kingdom
00120112 / $22.95

The Offspring – Greatest Hits
00690809 / $17.95

Jaco Pastorius – Greatest Jazz Fusion Bass Player
00690421 / $17.95

The Essential Jaco Pastorius
00690420 / $18.95

Pearl Jam – Ten
00694882 / $14.95

Pink Floyd – Dark Side of the Moon
00660172 / $14.95

The Best of Police
00660207 / $14.95

Pop/Rock Bass Bible
00690747 / $17.95

Queen – The Bass Collection
00690065 / $17.95

R&B Bass Bible
00690745 / $17.95

Rage Against the Machine
00690248 / $16.95

The Best of Red Hot Chili Peppers
00695285 / $24.95

Red Hot Chili Peppers – Blood Sugar Sex Magik
00690064 / $19.95

Red Hot Chili Peppers – By the Way
00690585 / $19.95

Red Hot Chili Peppers – Californication
00690390 / $19.95

Red Hot Chili Peppers – Greatest Hits
00690675 / $18.95

Red Hot Chili Peppers – One Hot Minute
00690091 / $18.95

Red Hot Chili Peppers – Stadium Arcadium
00690853 / $24.95

Red Hot Chili Peppers – Stadium Arcadium: Deluxe Edition
Book/2-CD Pack
00690863 / $39.95

Rock Bass Bible
00690446 / $19.95

Rolling Stones
00690256 / $16.95

System of a Down – Toxicity
00690592 / $19.95

Top Hits for Bass
00690677 / $14.95

Stevie Ray Vaughan – Lightnin' Blues 1983-1987
00694778 / $19.95

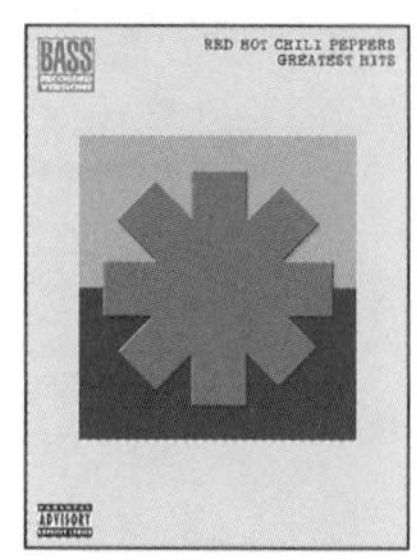

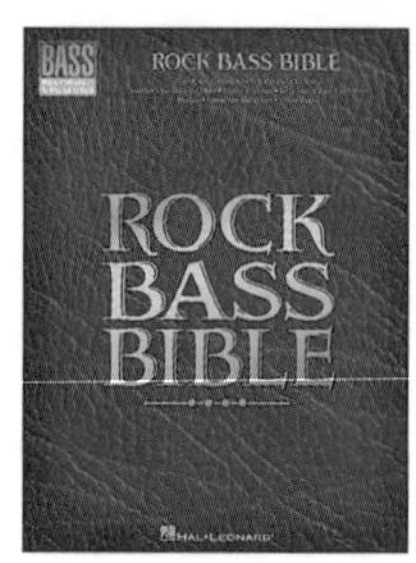

FOR MORE INFORMATION, SEE YOUR LOCAL MUSIC DEALER,
OR WRITE TO:

HAL•LEONARD® CORPORATION
7777 W. BLUEMOUND RD. P.O. BOX 13819 MILWAUKEE, WI 53213

Visit Hal Leonard Online at
www.halleonard.com

Prices, contents & availability subject to change without notice.
Some products may not be available outside the U.S.A.

0309

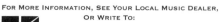